PRAISE FOR L
UNGRATEFUL DEAD

"So many parents have joined a club that no one wants to be a part of——the 'my child died of an overdose' club. For these families, grief is often overshadowed by shame. This book will resonate with so many families, as it explores Deborah's loss, her full-bodied love for her daughter, and the ever-lasting bond between the two of them, reminding the reader that addiction has nothing to do with morality..."

—*Emily Hage*, President & CEO First Call Alcohol/Drug Prevention & Recovery

———————————

"Deborah Shouse has blessed us with her brave and compassionate conversations with her daughter, Hilee, who died of a drug overdose. Thanks to the profound advice of her grief therapist, Deborah decided to write to Hilee and listen for her responses. These conversations are at once astounding, unbelievable—but believable—and also heartwarming and very hopeful."

—*Jane Murray, MD*

"*Letters From the Ungrateful Dead* is an emotional roller coaster shining a light on the pain of life, loss, and love. Deborah's writings are honest, raw, and share such deep and debilitating emotions mixed with humor in the depths of processing grief. This book will help many process the good, bad, and ugly that life can hand us; guiding us to find the deep riches of our authentic connections, no matter how imperfect we thought they were."

—**Lori La Bey,** Thought Leader and Founder of Alzheimer's Speaks and Dementia Map, Host of Alzheimer's Speaks Radio, and Author of *Betty the Bald Chicken – Lessons in How to Care.*

———————————

"At once a therapeutic exercise, a cathartic act, and an exceptional work of art, Shouse's book is a worthwhile read for anyone who's experienced the sudden and senseless demise of someone they dearly loved."

—**Ronald-Stéphane Gilbert,** Author of *Conversations with my Mother, A Novel of Love, Hope, and Dementia on the Maine Coast*

"This gripping collection of letters to and from Shouse's deceased daughter, Hilee, grabbed my attention on page one and held it until the very end. I read the book in one sitting! This sometimes humorous, sometimes heartbreaking book will undoubtedly help many other parents who are experiencing the grief of losing a child."

—*Marie Marley, PhD,* hospice volunteer and author of *Come Back Early Today: A Memoir of Love, Alzheimer's and Joy*

"*Letters From the Ungrateful Dead* is a captivating and heartwarming glimpse into the never-ending bond between mothers and their children. I laughed and shed more than one tear as I was transported inside their unconditional and loving relationship, knowing that their communication was authentic. A must-read for grieving parents seeking confirmation of their child's continued existence after bodily death."

—*Julie Ryan,* Psychic Medium and Medical Intuitive

"Deborah Shouse's *Letters from the Ungrateful Dead* is compelling, heart-wrenching, and beautifully written. She poignantly demonstrates that love is stronger than death."

—**Robert Brumet,** author of *Finding Yourself in Transition*

"Can we connect with our beloved dead? You won't forget Deborah Shouse's lovely, lyrical, often funny, and always heartfelt and heartbreaking quest to do just that. Don't be surprised if you are inspired to begin your own quiet correspondence with those you have loved and lost."

—**Andrea Warren,** author of *Enemy Child: The Story of Norman Mineta, a Boy Imprisoned in a Japanese American Internment Camp During World War II.*

"Whether one is a believer or not, death may end a life, but it does not end a relationship. This book is a spiritual testament to many truths. By writing to, and receiving letters from, her dead daughter, Shouse discovered in their relationship a kind of healing truth."

—*The Rev. Vern Barnet,* DMin, minister emeritus, The World Faiths Center for Religious Experience and Study

LETTERS FROM THE UNGRATEFUL DEAD

A GRIEVING MOM'S SURPRISING CORRESPONDENCE WITH HER DECEASED ADULT DAUGHTER

DEBORAH SHOUSE

Flint Hills Publishing

Letters from the Ungrateful Dead:
A Grieving Mom's Surprising
Correspondence with Her Deceased
Adult Daughter
© 2024 by Deborah Shouse

Cover Design by Amy Albright
stonypointgraphics.weebly.com

Flint Hills Publishing
Topeka, Kansas
Tucson, Arizona
www.flinthillspublishing.com

Printed in the U.S.A.

Paperback Book: ISBN: 978-1-953583-93-2
Electronic Book ISBN: 978-1-953583-95-6

Dedication

To my two daughters, Sarah and Hilee,
you are my heart.
To Hilee, with love and squalor.
To Sarah, with joy and ten thousand steps.

To my therapist, for the idea.

To my life partner Ron, for his steadfast
empathy and love.

To my brother Dan, for his weekly visits and his
decadent brownies.

Contents

Section 1

The
Inconceivable

Dear Reader:
A Note from Deborah

Every morning, I wake up early so I can write to my dead child. I say these cold words, "dead child," as a stark reminder that my daughter is gone. Saying "passed on," or "is no longer with us" leaves me too vulnerable to hope. She was 47 years old.

I write whatever is on my mind. Then I listen. So far, Hilee always answers. Her words appear in my head, reminding me she is no angel. At least, not yet.

Creating these notes to and from Hilee alleviates my burning sorrow. The more I write, the more connected I feel. Sometimes I type many letters a day. Sometimes just one. As I communicate with her, the past floods through me. My sorrows seep in, but Hilee's openness soothes me. Is it possible my daughter and I are finally experiencing our ideal relationship?

You, dear reader, might think, "Does Deborah really believe she's hearing from her deceased daughter? Doesn't she realize she's just writing to herself?" But, dear reader, I hear Hilee's voice, and her words and I transcribe them onto the page.

This book is a memorial to my daughter. I haven't included all of my letters, only the ones that seemed most meaningful and interesting. Although I wrote initially to ease my grief, I also wrote to better understand Hilee, her addictions, and her mental health challenges.

I wrote to explore myself, as a person and as a mother, and to untangle parts of our family dynamic. I wanted to be vulnerable and open about having a child who was not a traditional "success," but who was still an amazing and creative person.

Most important, I ached with missing my daughter and these letters kept her with me.

I missed Hilee so so much. Every day. Writing the letters gave me a way to stay in touch with her, to ask, to confess, to banter, to share. Writing let us unfold a new relationship, void of earthly constraints. Hilee wrote about herself and about me bluntly and frankly, without rancor. I grew to understand Hilee more deeply and I think she came to better understand me. Writing this has brought me immeasurable comfort and valuable insights, and I hope reading this will bring you comfort and insights as well.

Yours, Deborah

The End

My daughter's boyfriend Matthew calls at 11:30 p.m., crying, his words garbled. "Something is wrong with Hilee. She's not breathing. The EMTs are here."

"She can't be dead," is my first response, as my partner Ron and I speed to her house. By the time we get there, 20 minutes later, her street is clogged with emergency vehicles. Yellow crime scene tape surrounds her driveway. My younger daughter Sarah is already there, head bowed, tissue clutched. I hug Sarah, then float above myself as the detective, medical examiner, and police officer explain: my daughter, Hilee, is dead. This conversation is not real: I am observing someone else's life.

The detective tells us, "We are going to put the deceased in a body bag. You may not want to see this." He is shorter than I am and wears a bullet-proof vest. I follow his instructions and turn away. This body has nothing to do with my daughter. She is often a deep sleeper and can easily snooze through any kind of commotion.

"Was she suicidal?" the medical examiner asks.

"No. Not anymore. She was doing well."

Since her late teens, Hilee has struggled with borderline personality disorder, bipolar disorder, depression, and anxiety. For large swaths of her life, her threats of suicide pierced me. She'd tried to harm herself in many ways: cutting, burning, isolating, overmedicating, suddenly going off her medications, refusing to bathe or eat properly. She smoldered with anger and seethed with irritation. She was unable to hold a job and often loathe to leave her house. But in the last two years, she has been calmer. She takes her medications more consistently. She's fallen in love and talks about her future.

In earlier years, I had imagined her death and had seen myself a wailing banshee of grief, immobilized by loss.

Now, the medical examiner tells me. "She had already stopped breathing by the time we arrived. We did everything we could to bring her back to life."

I clench my hands, thank them. But I do not fall to the ground sobbing. Because she isn't really dead.

"We are confiscating her phone," the detective says. "There are used needles lying around everywhere inside her duplex. Hers could be a drug-related incident. Her texts could lead us to the dealer. But we won't have definitive information until we get the autopsy report."

My mind races: Dealer? Drugs? Needles? Autopsy report? Only people in TV crime series have autopsies. Not my child.

It is 1:30 a.m. and Hilee lies on her lawn, in a body bag, waiting for a ride to the coroner's.

I know Hilee smokes pot and sometimes overuses her multitude of prescription drugs. But I never imagined she was using hard drugs.

Earlier this evening, Hilee texted me, explaining she desperately needed a new cell phone and had found one on sale. She didn't sound like someone who would be dead in four hours. Now, the police are seizing that old phone. I am grateful that I'd promised to look into that bargain. Very grateful. Would the detective read my reply and think, "What a good mother Deborah is."

The morning after Hilee's death, I open my refrigerator and take out an apple. I am numb as I go outside, amazed I am able to move around. In the past, days could go by without a text or call from Hilee. After five days, my worry would crescendo and I'd call Sarah, asking, "Have you talked to her?"

"No, have you?"

"No. Shall we do anything? Shall we go over there, bang on the door?"

"If we don't hear from her by tomorrow, then yes…"

The next day, I'd call and Hilee would answer. She knows our limits, understands when I am knotted into anxiety and about to burst. Probably this time will be the same. Just when I'm in utter despair, she'll call.

Meanwhile, friends and family cocoon me. They are standing by in case I don't hear from Hilee, in case the detective, the coroner, and the medical examiner are right and my daughter. is. really. dead.

The Beginning

The days after Hilee's death are a blur as I try to understand this immeasurable loss. For six weeks, I don't know her cause of death. When the autopsy report finally arrives, it's a punch in the gut: overdose of meth and fentanyl.

I flounder through several months. Then a friend recommends Eve, a grief therapist. I am so ready for help. In our first session, Eve says, "Why don't you write letters to Hilee and have her write you back?"

"Write me back?" The concept seems utterly bizarre. "How do I know what Hilee will say?"

"Quiet your mind and let her voice come through."

The idea seems absurd, but I am desperate for connection with my daughter.

So, the next morning, I wake up early and slump on the living room sofa with my laptop. The sparrows and finches are darting around our bird feeders and their cheerful chatting almost makes me smile. But a heavy sadness presses on my forehead. My mind is numb, my fingers stiff.

I make myself write:

Dear Hilee,

It's very strange to go all these days, weeks, and months without talking to you. I don't like it. Even this Thanksgiving, I missed you and all the sad, depressed, crying calls you usually make during this difficult season.

Love, Mom

Then I close my eyes and my tears travel. I keep my hands on the keyboard and listen. I hear Hilee's voice in my head:

Dear Mom,

I'm glad you finally wrote! Up here, or wherever I am, they want you to think about a lot of spiritual stuff. I didn't do that when I was alive. Why would I start now? They have streaming, but all the shows are self-help stuff. No zombie movies at all, which is too bad.

About Thanksgiving, what a relief. They don't have holidays here. Maybe they don't even have days. I wasn't listening when we had that orientation session.

Please keep in touch. There are no Amazon or Etsy deliveries, so I never get any mail.

Love, Hilee

Her charm, cynicism, combativeness, sly sense of humor, and her need to be loved come through. I write down everything she says. After all these months, it's astonishing to feel like she's talking to me. When she stops speaking, I bow my head and cover my mouth with my hands. For those moments, I have my daughter back.

All that day, images and memories of Hilee flood me. They dance, they spar, they shout, they sing. During the night, they poke me, slapping away my sleep. So I get up, go downstairs, and write.

Dear Hilee,

I have not eaten at Johnny Cascone's restaurant since you died. I think of calling our favorite waitress and ordering my eggplant meal, but I know she'll ask about you and I'd have to tell her that you're dead. I can't do that.

I'd like to eat there with someone who would order your usual meal of chicken parmesan with extra sugo sauce, their special hash brown potatoes, Diet Coke, and lemon cake for dessert.

Love, Mom

Instantly, Hilee responds.

Mom,

I'm glad you didn't eat at Cascone's without me. I loved that food so much and I particularly liked figuring out what to order with Matthew. Oh my goodness, we had such big conversations about it. The food tasted better when I shared it with Matthew. Even before we fell in love, we had an amazing time analyzing that menu.

Perhaps you should have a meal there because you'd be thinking about me with every bite.

And that would mean we'd be spending time together. Even though we're terribly far apart, even farther apart than when I lived in LA.

Would you believe, they have dogs here? Yes, and they don't poop or pee or get hungry or need to go on walks. They are perfectly attuned, so when you need a cuddle, a dog comes trotting over. And when you're restless, they run off and play with someone else. The dogs are one very good thing about this being dead business. Still, I miss Muddy, even though I know he has a good home, with a big yard and a Collie for company.

They also have softy blankies here, with a silky strip across the top, just like you used to get for me. You can have as many as you want, but I decided to stop at three.

I am doodling again. They have an excellent selection of markers and nice art paper. The supplies appear when I think about them. Given the lame TV programs, it's almost as much fun to draw.

With love and death, Hilee

So begins our surprising correspondence, an increasingly authentic and vulnerable communication that Hilee and I could achieve only randomly when she was alive. Writing and reading our letters anchors me and offers me solace during a terrible and tumultuous time of immense grief. The letters are my lifeline.

Writing to My Daughter and Inviting Her to Write Back

How to Create an After-Life Correspondence

At first, the suggestion of writing to my deceased child seemed impossible. Hilee had always communicated with me on her terms. She was never consistent. She could ignore me for days or she might bombard me with 17 calls in one hour, depending on her mood and her need. She texted me frequently, but rarely wrote an actual note or letter.

I was desperate to connect with her and my grief therapist's instructions were calm and simple: Find a quiet space and start writing to Hilee. Then, close my eyes, take a breath, and listen for Hilee's voice in my head.

I did just that. Miraculously, I heard my daughter talk to me and I wrote down everything she said. What a relief! I felt instantly connected from that initial experience.

I usually wrote in the morning, after awakening, when my mind was clear. I sat alone in our living room, on a cranberry-colored futon, with my fingers resting on my laptop keyboard, and poured out whatever was on my mind. Then I waited, hands poised, for Hilee's response. For the first time in our relationship, she showed up every time and always had something to say. As I wrote, our pet guinea pigs, Juno and Coco, rustled around in their nearby habitat, munching hay, drinking water, then curling up for a rest. Their innocent presence was a comfort.

When my mind was foggy, or I was too sad to focus, I took a walk and spoke to Hilee. Naturally, she did not answer, being a woman averse to outdoor movement. But talking out loud to myself was helpful. Often, that short stroll cleared my mind and allowed me to go home and reach out to Hilee.

Even though writing to Hilee diminished my sense of loss, it often intensified my sadness. I was sometimes grouchy or hyper-sensitive after writing. I had to practice letting those feelings course through me before I stepped into the rest of my day. Sometimes I boosted my spirits by doing other writing, exercising, or talking to a friend. Other times I ate dark chocolate and moped around for a while. (Which I'm not necessarily recommending as a prime coping skill, although it does have its merits.)

For months, I wrote to Hilee daily, often several times a day. Hearing from Hilee kept me from missing her quite so much. I had worried she'd be forgotten, and the letters felt like a memorial to her. Because she wasn't burdened by her depression, anger, and anxiety, communicating with her felt meaningful and companionable. We were airing our differences and explaining our viewpoints in a safe and authentic way.

In addition to the catharsis of corresponding with Hilee, I also benefitted from reading and rereading our letters. Through that process, I grew into a deeper understanding of my relationship with Hilee, her struggles and triumphs, as well as my own foibles and strengths. I shared selected letters with my therapist and with friends and relatives. They all thanked me for inviting them to read these intimate missives, saying they'd gained insight into Hilee and were also moved by my grieving process.

I hope my experiences can help you reconnect with your loved one, easing your sorrow, tackling unfinished business, and keeping your loved one's spirit in the here and now.

Section 11

Letters
from the
Ungrateful
Dead

December, the Dreaded "First" Holidays Without Hilee

I found my grief therapist in mid-November and started writing to Hilee two weeks later. The holidays were always a hard time for Hilee, and she was often grouchy, angry, or depressed. Our correspondence during this challenging season helped me feel connected to her. I loved pouring out my heart at odd hours of the day or night, knowing she would write me back. After 47 years, Hilee and I started getting to know each other in a new way.

Dear Hilee,

Sarah and I miss you so much. "Inconceivable." Isn't that what Wallace Shawn says so often in the *Princess Bride?* That's the way I feel about your death.

Last night I dreamed you popped into my room, very alive. I was surprised, excited to see you. And I was confused.

"Where have you been?" I asked.

"Oh, here and there," you said.

You told me you'd gotten sick of life, and you'd decided to disappear. You were so casual, like you didn't realize all the sorrow and grief I've been through. I pressed my lips together, wanting to shout at you.

"You owe me a lot of money," I said instead, listing the cremation costs, the lawyer's fees....

Then I woke up.

Hmmmm...

Mom

Dear Mom,

Really? You talked to me about money after I mercifully returned from the dead in your dreams? Remind me not to do that again!

Plus, surely you know I'll never pay you back!

Mom, who else do you know who can communicate without a computer, cell phone, or internet? I'm definitely one with "the cloud."

We have a TV channel called Stuff on Earth. It's pretty cool, kind of like if Google Maps could gossip. I can tune into any city, any neighborhood, even hone in on a house. I can think about an address and see what's going on there. It's not just Santa who can "see you when you're sleeping!"

Love, Spy in the Sky, Hilee

Dear Hilee,

That spy in the sky stuff is a bit disturbing.

I am now grateful you rarely showed up for holiday dinners. That way, I'm not so burdened with warm glowing memories of celebrating Chanukah with you. But I am burdened with other memories, both tender and dark. Discussing what gifts you wanted, mainly money or Amazon gift cards, you always wanted more than I wanted to give. Love and money were intertwined in your psyche. It was a challenge to negotiate an amount that allowed you to feel loved.

Most years, you promised to come to Chanukah family dinner, then hours before the meal, you'd call with a cold or cough or headache or depression. I dreaded hearing the phone ring. I dreaded that gut-twist of disappointment. I should have known better than to get excited about celebrating with you, but I always, always hoped. Isn't that what Chanukah's all about: a time of unexpected miracles?

At least you were ecumenical: you usually skipped out on your Dad's family's Christmas gathering as well.

Love, Mom

Dear Mom,

Aren't all miracles unexpected? Wasn't that Chanukah fuss over some plain old olive oil that lasted a couple of days longer than expected?

Anyway, yes, you should have known I wouldn't show up. But all the same, I'm sorry you went through that. I'm sorry I couldn't buck up and show up. I couldn't. I really couldn't. I had to accept it and I think you're starting to accept it.

That's another plus about being dead: having an excused absence from almost everything. Except maybe a seance.

Love, The Hilee that Stole Chanukah

Dear Hilee,

Robert and I have been playing a game you'd like—Bananagrams. It's like a relaxing semi-Scrabble. No points. No board. You're just creating linked words. If you get to return to Earth, we'll have to play. Do you ever return? Even for a short visit?

Last night we made a casserole from spaghetti squash, fake cheese, vegan sour cream, and vegetables. You would not be surprised to learn it wasn't delicious. We ate it—but definitely not worth making again.

Love, Mom

Dear Mom,

Why don't you use real gooey cow-made cheese and sumptuous dairy-laden sour cream? Then that wretched squash might have tasted like something.

Remember back in junior high when I became a vegetarian? It was so cool that you and Sarah became vegetarians too. I was the leader of our family in that way. And look, even though I've long been eating pork chops and hamburgers, you're still eating those plants. Amazing!

Love, Hilee the Carnivore, grrr

Dear Hilee,

You were absolutely the leader for our vegetarian phase. I was relieved, actually. Even back then, I didn't enjoy eating meat. When I went out to eat with Larry and friends, I felt I had to order steak like the rest of the group. Then I'd cut the meat into tiny bites and hide it under my mashed potatoes.

Last night on TV, one of the character's father died. The guy carried his dad's ashes to the ocean to spread them. I thought about your ashes in our back room and all the energy left my body. I was totally empty.

I have a plan to drift some of your ashes into the parking lots of your favorite restaurants. I haven't done it yet because I don't really believe you are dead.

With love but no ashes, Mom

Dear Mom,

Dead or whatever I am, I'm definitely in an alternative universe. I like your idea of the ashes at my restaurants. Not nearly as sentimental and gooey as dumping them in the ocean. As if I'd go near the ocean! Let me know what you decide. Or maybe I'll activate my I Spy powers and learn for myself. Maybe I'm psychic now and I'll know before you do! I still haven't read the owner's manual or whatever book they keep "encouraging" me to look at.

Love, Hilee

Dear Hilee,

I can't decide whether I should just pull myself together and get on with life or if I should languish and wallow in my sadness.

Can you float? Do you walk around or fly? Any special superpowers you have now that you're "out of this world?"

You always loved science fiction. Your dad introduced me to science fiction. I'd never read any of it, nor any Isaac Singer either, until I met Larry. When I was in love with him, I was brimming with admiration over his fabulous intellect. You have the same kinds of intelligence!

Love, Mom

Dear Mom,

I spy with my little eye—

I may have a few superpowers. Like the other day, I was walking around and I tripped. I should have fallen but I bounced and floated instead.

I'm secretly hoping I can fly, but I'm not ready to try it because I don't want to be horribly disappointed if I can't. I don't think I can turn water into wine or anything Biblical like that, but I may be able to turn Coke into Diet Coke. Yes, can you believe it, they have only water and regular soda here? I asked one of the floating guides for a Diet Coke and he (or she, I can't tell) said, "For that you have to go to Hell."

I don't know if he meant that literally and I don't know how to get to Hell's convenience store. I mean, just because I'm dead doesn't mean I suddenly like to walk around, talk to strangers, and explore new things.

Yeah, I read a lot of books because of Dad. Science fiction, of course. Isaac Singer, of course. But I also had to read Dad's favorite political philosopher, Hannah Arendt. I bet you didn't read her.

By the way, there's no library here per se, but you can visualize any book and it appears. Even if you just think of it for a minute. So, it's a problem, because I am surrounded by mountains of books whose titles just crashed into my mind. I don't know how to get rid of them. Probably in the manual, huh?   Love Hilee

Dear Mom,

A big plus about being dead: I am not anxious or panicked. I am not depressed. I am calm. Of course, that means life's not too interesting, but I am trying to be in the flow and see if I can tolerate it.

It's hard to stir up drama here. Everyone is sanguine. Or enlightened. Oh God, what if I'm becoming enlightened! You are entitled to make fun of me if that happens.

Remember how I scorned all your suggestions to breathe, think positively, create affirmations, vision my life. I thought those things were so stupid. Then I went to that cognitive behavior therapy class. They were into that and since I had to do my homework—I was trying to be more normal—I started doing affirmations. It wasn't as bad as I thought.

Love, Hilee

Dear Hilee,

I had such hopes that the behavior classes would help you. I always expected great results the few times you agreed to therapy.

Love, Mom

Dear Mom,

You always wanted to change me.

Bad idea.   Love, Hilee

Dear Hilee,

I always wanted you to be happy. Happier at least. But yes, I thought you'd need to change for that to happen.

The other factor—I am Jewish and I am a mother. Therefore, I am a Jewish mother. I can't help it! It's my job to want you to be happy. And try to fix it if you are not. My legacy. My duty.

Love, Mom

Dear Mom,

Ha ha ha! It's in your Jewishy mother genes, right! It could always be worse, right?

Love, Hilee

January, the New Year Dares Me to Step Into It

I am getting more comfortable jumping into painful or difficult topics. For me and Hilee, this open communication is relatively new territory. Her revelations and insights are both sobering and illuminating. I wonder how she feels about mine?

Dear Hilee,

Remember when you went to the tattoo parlor and paid to get professional scars? No more of the do-it-yourself cutting you'd been randomly doing since you were thirteen. Now your scars were going to be art instead of cries of pain.

You were 33 and had just lost your job. You spent $100 of your unemployment check on an ankle scar. It was quite raw looking, and you wanted me to touch it. I almost threw up, but I did touch it with the tip of my finger.

Hilee, you tried many different ways to modify your body. Tattoos. Piercing. You had so many interesting pierces. Then scarification. The scarring was the hardest for me to accept.

When you were five years old, you and I, along with Sarah in her stroller, were walking through Crown Center on a toy-shopping trip. A teenage girl dressed in goth black, with dyed black hair, big silver nose piercings, and evil dragon tattoos overwhelming her bare arms, slouched past us.

"My daughters will never look and dress like that," I murmured.

Ha ha ha! So much for self-righteous proclamations. Eight years later, you had a pile of black clothes on your bedroom floor and your first tattoo. With many more to follow. It took me a while to appreciate your skin art, to understand that the inked symbols were about you, reclaiming your body. Not about me being a bad mother.

Love, Mom

Dear Mom,

You can't understand the intensity of scarring. It's horrific and thrilling at the same time. It's destruction that turns into beauty, like burning lava slashing through a village, and leaving behind ghostly mountains. And the piercing—I had so many lovely secret pierces. Remember when I needed to have an MRI and you took me to the tattoo place so they could remove all my piercings? And the guy was so nice, he didn't even charge me!

Love, Hilee

Dear Hilee,

You were quite at home and personable at the tattoo place. I was very impressed. But I was always impressed when you used your charisma. Like a peacock, suddenly displaying his glorious tail feathers. You are great at warmly connecting with people. Alas, you are equally great at brutally shoving people away. Do you agree?

Love, Mom

Dear Mom,

Well, I wouldn't call it "brutally" shoving, but yes, essentially, I agree. I tried to push people away before they pushed me. I didn't want to be rejected. Of course, now that I'm up here and not in the middle of everyday life, I do wonder if I overdid the pushing business. Maybe people really liked me and wanted to be friends with me?

Curious, Hilee

Dear Hilee,

Yes, especially people like Sarah and me. We definitely liked you and wanted to be friends with you. You had a lot happen to you when you were alive, Hilee. You were doing your best.

Love, Mom

Dear Hilee,

It has been six months since you texted me that you needed a new phone. That was our last Earthly communication. Five hours later, Matthew called screaming, "Something is wrong with Hilee!" You probably were already dead. Dead. I still do not believe it, Hilee. I miss you immeasurably.

Remember the old image of the girl plucking the tender white petals from a daisy, reciting, "Loves me, Loves me not," with each discard. My refrain: "She's alive. She's alive not."

Yes, after almost six months, I still do not fully believe you are dead. In my file cabinet, the scarlet secret of your demise, the autopsy report, shouts, "Overdose of meth and fentanyl."

You haven't called me in six months, perhaps because the police confiscated your cellphone. I still await your call because it is impossible that my daughter of 47 years is no longer alive. Just forming the thought, my throat is full of holes. My mouth is sour with sorrow. My eyes cannot see into the distance.

I slump on the sofa, immobilized. And yet, moments, perhaps hours later, I rise. I always rise.

Love, YJM (Your Jewish Mother)

Dear Mom,

I miss you too. I didn't really understand how dangerous the drugs were: I just wanted to feel happy. I thought I would just relax until Matthew came home and we'd have dinner together. I thought the two of us would be living together for quite a while, a team. We loved each other. I fell into what I thought was an ordinary sleep. Then I woke up here, without my dog, my house, my boyfriend, my Diet Coke, my cigarettes, my remote. With nothing.

Did I tell you that you get to pick out your own clothes here? You don't even have to order on Etsy — you just imagine an outfit and it's on you, fitting perfectly. I wish I had my phone so I could send you some pictures. I look great!

Today, I am wearing sequined jeans, low rider, and a purple tank top, like the one I got at the thrift store, only more elegant. And I don't have to bargain shop or worry about money. Who knows how much this outfit costs? Plus, you can have hair and makeup done at any time. It only takes minutes. Can you tell, I'm finally wandering around some, checking things out.

If I were back home, we'd go to Sprouts today and Cascone's. Or maybe, I'd call you and cancel—ha ha ha! Some things never change.

With love and squalor and
death and sparkling jeans, YJD
(Your Jewish Daughter) Hilee

Dear Hilee,

Sarah and I went for a walk last night and talked about how unbelievable it is that you're not here. You're not in your duplex on Grandview Lane. You're not calling us, desperate to persuade us to go to Wal-Mart to pick up your meds. You are not texting because you need a Diet Coke or a ride to the doctor or you're out of food — you're not really out of food but you may need fish sticks for dinner or a Kit Kat for dessert.

I miss those calls, some more than others, of course. Remember how mad you could get if we failed to instantly fetch you what you needed? Still, it must have been frustrating that you couldn't drive because of your random seizures. You had to rely on "the kindness of strangers," as they say. And of family members.

Love, Mom

Dear Mom,

No meds is another good thing about being dead. I practically have a degree in pharmacology from all the drugs I've juggled through the years. Half the time I was advising the psychiatrist on the medications I needed.

In a way, I miss being angry. When you're mad, you know you're alive. You feel powerful, righteous, in charge. At least I did. And being angry helped me get what I wanted. With Dad at least. And sometimes with you. Oh well, those times are gone. Maybe I don't miss them so much.

How long am I going to be here, do you know? I'm wondering if I should get used to it, try to make friends? Or should I just chill, in case I'm leaving soon?

One of the floating islands—that's what I call the creatures that glide around answering questions and offering help—told me there's a video I could watch, rather than reading that manual. Maybe I'll do that. Maybe.

Love, Hilee

Dear Hilee,

On today's walk, I talked to you. Did you hear me? Is there a little ding, like a text, that alerts you when someone is thinking about you?

I wasn't pretending we were walking together: I would never do that, knowing how you feel about exercise. I was musing about our early lives, wondering if you were happy part of that time—I think you were, but maybe I was just oblivious to what you were going through.

Here's something you would like: Ron and I went

to Dan and Dena's tonight for dinner and had six desserts. Three of them were samples of a healthy protein-type bar that included "real chocolate." We ate bites of peanut butter, fudge, and almond crunch. Then Dan offered a home-baked peanut butter cookie and a chocolate peanut butter cookie. Dena contributed a bonbon from a fancy chocolatier in Boulder. You would have enjoyed sampling everything. Plus, Dan sent us home with leftovers.

Love, Mom

Dear Mom,

Sometimes I get a sense that you've written but I may be resting or daydreaming or designing a new outfit in my head, and I don't want to communicate. You don't mind, do you?

Those desserts sound like fun, but maybe a bit too fancy and fibrous for me. I prefer Hershey bars, store-bought apple pies, and donuts oozing with filling.

Mom, here's something you need to know: you have never understood depression. You're too bouncy and shiny. Even though you are a great person, a nice person, nicer than I ever deserved, you have never felt the weight of this condition. You do not understand that eating a sprig of broccoli and walking around the block is not possible when a hundred-ton dinosaur is sitting on you, ranting about how useless you are.

When I was in that space, everything you said translated into criticism and blame, even though part of me realized you were trying to help. Okay, I may be exaggerating about the broccoli. But you get the idea. Anyhow, I wanted to clear that up. I'm pretty sure you won't agree with me.

In case you're interested, here are my superpowers so far:

• Bouncing instead of falling, although I really don't care for bouncing.

• Being my own fashion designer and manifesting my own clothes.

• Going without glasses. Maybe there's nothing to see here or maybe I just see everything clearly in my mind. Remember how I often lost or broke my glasses and you had to take me to Target for an eye exam?

• Sometimes, knowing when people are thinking about me. At least I hope it's only sometimes, because my boyfriend Matthew isn't paying enough attention to me. I'm thinking of putting a little curse on him or appearing as a ghost to frighten him, but I don't know how to do either of those. I know what you're going to say: "Read the manual, watch the video, already." Or maybe I'll meet a dead witch and she'll assist me. That's the way I usually find out stuff, run into someone who can help me. I wonder if they have a Facebook page for dead people. Now *that* I might look into.

Love, H

Dear Hilee,

You are right: I have not experienced depression the way you have. But I truly believe that some healthy habits can ease the pain of it.

What can I say? I believe I'm right, and I never give up.

You believe you are right, and you never give up. I guess we're related.

I'm glad you're listing your superpowers. It's exciting to have even one. Keep me posted and let me know when you meet your mentoring witch.

I often think of the bad witch in the Wizard of Oz, crying out, "I'm melting!" Did you feel like you were melting when you died? Or maybe you didn't even notice until afterwards.

Love, GlenDeb, the Good Witch

Dear Hilee,

I believe this is our longest correspondence ever. We didn't write letters when you were living in L.A., did we? We talked on the phone and most of the time, you were so unhappy. Your beloved boyfriend was off to L.A. for a Master's Degree and you insisted on joining him. He was skeptical, but you persisted. It was a disaster for you both. You'd never been so far from home. You started hallucinating. You phoned me crying almost every day. I tried to soothe you, to encourage you, to remind you how strong you are. But you were in a high state of panic and couldn't listen.

You were so excited when you finally pried yourself out of the apartment and walked to the convenience store down the block. You did it! You left the apartment! We celebrated that rare and mighty accomplishment over the telephone.

Love, Mom

Dear Mom,

Oh God, I remember that horrible time. I thought pure love could keep us together, but it turned out I needed good mental health and rational thinking as well. Having a job and being willing to cook dinner wouldn't have hurt. Who knew?

Remember how I told you there was no Diet Coke here, only regular soda? Well, wherever there are people, or "beings formerly known as people," there are the things those people want!

Now that I'm exploring my environment, I'm running into several alternative beings, otherwise known as unsavory characters, and possibly drug addicts. It makes me wonder if I am in a neighborhood of "former" addicts.

Isn't that a form of discrimination?

Anyhow, it suits me fine. One of these characters has clued me into Convenience on the Edge. I'm not sure what "Edge" they're referring to—Edge of Hell, Edge of Reason, Edge of Night—I didn't ask. The shop is like a miniature 7-11 with a lot of boot-legged products. Some creative creature figured out how to suck the regular sugar out of Coke and replace it with whatever addictive artificial sweetener makes Diet Coke wickedly compelling. So today—drum roll—I had my first out-of-body Diet Coke derivative. It was, as they say down where you are, a heavenly experience.

Love, Your Incorrigible Daughter, H

Dear Hilee,

I might have known you'd figure out how to get your Diet Coke.

You always manage to get what you want. Remember when you were dying to attend the National Crossword Puzzle Tournament and you talked me into paying for the adventure and even weaseled me and Sarah into going with you? You were so excited. But during our first afternoon in New York, your good spirits evaporated, and you suddenly turned mean. You said, "I hate you and I'm sorry I came!" We were walking to Tix to pick out a Broadway show for the evening, and we all stopped and stood on the sidewalk, staring at each other.

I wanted to shout, "Then just go home!" But I bit my lip and swallowed those bitter words. Still, I was disappointed you couldn't enjoy even one day of your dream trip.

We kept walking, clouded by an uneasy silence. Then we heard, "Deborah Shouse. Deborah Shouse!" I looked around and saw a Kansas City playwright friend walking toward us. He told us he had a play off-Broadway, and he'd been at a rehearsal.

We congratulated him and after he left, Sarah said, "I didn't realize you knew a famous playwright, Mom."

We all laughed at my elevated status, and I felt better. You and Sarah selected *Beauty and the Beast* for our theatrical experience, and it was magical. The next day, we took a bus to New Jersey and the Crossword Puzzle tournament. Once there, you were social, charming, and outgoing. It turned out to be a great trip after all.

Love, Mom

Dear Mom,

That was a thrilling trip. I even made several friends.

For the record, I probably didn't really hate you. I was just stressed being around so many people. And it's good to know you didn't hate me, even after I said that to you.

I'm beginning to think you really did love me. I know you tried to convince me that you loved me, but I always felt you were being polite. You are very polite, which is irritating. I'm much more comfortable with people blurting out stuff and then apologizing for being rude.

Sorry if I hurt your feelings. I really did like the trip.

And now look how far I've come. Literally. Probably thousands of miles at least.

Love, H

Dear Mom,

There's nothing to worry about here! No one to get angry at, no one to argue or fight with. What is the point?

One of the floating guides told me I was lucky to be here. Another advised me to get a hobby. Can you imagine someone saying the word "hobby" to me?

Guess what! I met the genius who created the other-worldly brand of Diet Coke. He's like a shaking skeleton with lots of tattoos, torn jeans, and a flannel shirt with a tough-looking leather jacket. His teeth are even worse than mine—chewing tobacco probably. He also died of an overdose. Heroin with fentanyl. But he was a long-time drug user. I mean, for a while, he had a gold case he carried his needles in. Where did he get the money for that, you may wonder? Selling drugs, of course.

He's giving me free Diet Coke, which doesn't really mean anything because there's no money or credit cards here. Yesterday, I met him near the Edge on some old wooden benches, and we chatted about everything. No secrets. Now I'm starting to see what the floating guides mean about rejuvenation—it felt great, drinking a "Diet Coke," no ice, smoking a cigarette, and talking about drugs and sex, and other dark arts. Although maybe those guides were thinking green juice, mud wraps, hot yoga, and singing crystal bowls. (Are you surprised I know about the singing bowls? I thought that would impress you).

So Mom, I may have my first dead friend.

Morbidly, Hilee

Dear Hilee,

Congratulations on making a friend. You are always so good at that when you're in the mood. He sounds like a combination of your previous boyfriends. Are you two plotting a zombie return to earth? Maybe you could visit as a semi-friendly ghost first. Your friend is welcome as well. I bet he hasn't read the training manual either.

I have a photo of you and Sarah when you were teaching yourself the Tae Bo workout. My goodness, you look great. So does Sarah. Despite the difficulties in your life, you had some good and great moments.

Love, Mom

Dear Mom,

Damn straight he hasn't read the manual. And he's proud of it!

Love, H

Dear Hilee,

When I started to fall in love with your dad, he told me he was one quarter Jewish. He also claimed to be one quarter Cherokee. My mother was happy to hear about the Jewish portion. But she was not wild about his big, brilliant personality and his ardent adoration of me. While he was sweeping me off my feet, Mom was trying to nail me to the ground. But, as you know, her strategy did not work.

One day, after Larry and I were married, I was in his mom's kitchen helping peel potatoes, and I asked her about the Jewish side of her family. Your grandmother was a big, sturdy, no-nonsense woman, with a razor-edged sense of privacy and an intolerance for chatter. She looked at me like I'd danced around her cooking space with dog dung on my shoes.

"There are no Jews," she said. "We're Baptists, from way back."

"And your Cherokee mother?"

She gave me a disdainful glance. Either it wasn't true, or she didn't want to talk about it.

I kept peeling. Then I asked about her mom's summertime gardens. That plunged us into a conversation on the merits of Big Boy and Best Boy tomatoes.

In case you ever wonder, your grandmother favored the Big Boys. I was so sad she died before you were born. She was prickly and stern, but she would have loved you.

Mom

Dear Mom,

What a story. I imagine Grandma Garnetta and I would have gotten along fine, at least until I started goofing off in school. Dad probably thought he'd get extra points if he belonged to a persecuted minority instead of being just another white guy.

He was totally a chameleon, able to argue both sides of most issues, which he often did just to be contrary. It took me ages to figure out how to win an argument with him.

Love, H

Dear Hilee,

I never figured out how to win an argument. What was your technique? Not that it matters, now that he's dead.

Love, Mom

Dear Mom,

I won my arguments with Dad by whining, pestering, manipulating, crying, and threatening not to run his errands. Back then, I had a car. Who else was going to drive to the store at 3:00 a.m. to get him chocolate!

His weapons were withholding—money and love, primarily—along with shaming, including, "I'm going to be dead someday and you'll be sorry YOU WEREN'T NICER TO ME."

But he was wrong: when he died I was so so so sad. But I wasn't sorry about much. I wanted my way; he wanted his. The wheedling, persuading, browbeating was part of our relationship; it meant he loved me.

I haven't seen Dad up here. But I imagine we're hanging out in different neighborhoods.

Love, H

Dear Hilee,

What do you suppose Larry would have thought of your ex, Carlton? Would the two of them have been friends?   Love, Mom

Dear Mom

Hah! Dad would have hated anyone I might have loved better than him. He would have tried to persuade me not to marry him. But that wouldn't have stopped me. Right?

Love, Hilee

Dear Hilee,

Generally speaking, you can't stop someone who's in love. I was certainly adamant when I fell in love with Larry. The thought of being without him was impossible. My parents tried to convince me that he was not a suitable person and that I was too young to get married. I wouldn't listen: he was getting drafted into the Army and we simply had to be together.

But with Carlton, I had no desire to dissuade you. First, I knew you'd never listen to me. Second, Carlton's adoration of you was compelling. And you loved him. The marrying part seemed a bit much to me, but you both really wanted it. Maybe you wanted the attention and the presents more than the til-death-do-us-part concept?

Love, Mom

Dear Mom,

I certainly enjoy presents, that's for sure. And I got a lot of them because of Carlton's mom throwing that big shower for me and all her friends coming. And she liked me, she really did. Although at the end, or even in the middle, Carlton told her a lot of rotten things and she wouldn't speak to me.

Love, Hilee, the Debonaire and
Sometimes Depressed Divorcee

Dear Hilee,

That's one thing in my favor: I always speak to you, even when things are tough. Are you still holding grudges against me? I wonder if I have any grudges against you?

For so many years, you were furious at me for checking you into the psych ward when you were thirteen. I have already apologized many times and explained why I admitted you: I thought you were going to try to kill yourself again. So did your therapist. So did mine. I couldn't keep you safe and I thought you would die.

All these years later, I turned out to be sadly right. Even though you didn't intentionally kill yourself, I couldn't keep you safe.

Love, Mom

Dear Mom,

I've mostly forgiven you, but not totally. You have to admit, you may have overreacted a bit back then.

Love, Hilee

Dear Hilee,

I was absolutely terrified I would lose you. I don't regret trying to keep you alive.

Remember the high school theater production you starred in? You played an angry woman, and you were amazing, so realistic. It was relaxing to see you angry on a stage and not at me.

Love, Mom

Dear Mom,

I saw Lothar again, the tough-looking guy who doctored up the Diet Coke. Before he became a rich corporate exec, then quit everything to immerse himself in alcohol and drugs, he worked on his grandfather's farm in the summers.

Due to his early agricultural experiences, he's figured out how to grow pot here! This guy is a genius. Since there is no dirt, he harnessed the moisture in the nearby clouds and voila, he's got tokes.

We sat on the corner near the Edge and smoked. It was wonderful. Who knows what he'll come up with next. You have to admire someone who doesn't even pretend he wants to quit drinking or using. Well, maybe you don't, but I do.

By the way, his name isn't really Lothar. He had a regular name, like Richard, when he was alive. In fact, he told me *Forbes* magazine did an article about him when he died. He wasn't bragging, just talking.

Anyway, he decided he needed a dead name. I didn't even have to look up the meaning of Lothar—the answer zapped into my head: it means "renowned warrior" in German.

Do you think I should come up with a dead name? Malomar? Vernacity? Creepsicle? Darkheart? Witch Hazel?

Love, Hilee, the Unnamed

Dear Hilee,

I'd like to see you. Would it be like that old movie *Harvey*, with the giant invisible rabbit, where you'd be with me, but only I would know you were there?

As far as a dead name, Verushka has a certain spine-tingling charm.

Love, Mom

Dear Mom,

Did the police ever give back my cell? Did they even have the right to take it? It had a lot of cute pictures of me and Matthew in it.

Mom, everyday-life seems so far away—kind of like *Yesterday*. I can't believe I stayed around for 47 years. I always intended to leave early, but I never could get it together to do myself in. Plus, I didn't want to make you and Sarah sad.

I am trying for a name more commanding than Verushka—such as Mordorimore.

Love, Hilee Mordy Shouse

Dear Hilee,

Yesterday I heard an end-of-life doctor on the radio. She helps families when their loved ones pass away. If she has to do an autopsy, she'll give the deceased a blanket if it makes the family feel better. She lets the family sit with the body before cremation.

I burst into tears when I heard this—I tried so hard to get you some post-death comfort. I wanted to sit with you, but the morgue rules wouldn't allow it. I felt so horrible that you were alone in there. Even now, it hurts my heart to think of it.

Sadly, Mom

Dear Mom,

No worries, Mom. My last moments on Earth, I was drifting into sleep. Then, I was here and confused. But not for long, because some being instantly brought me a dog and a blanket.

I appreciate your efforts, but I was already "in a better place," as some say. And who knows, maybe it's true. I am definitely in a "different" place.

Love, Hillie

Dear Mom,

I can concentrate again. I can read and remember what I read, just like I could before I was taking so many medications. I'm rereading all of Stephen King, in chronological order. After King, I'm reading all of Dad's favorite sci-fi, starting with Heinlein. Then I may turn to Anne Rice.

I haven't tried flying yet, but I want to. I'm thinking I'd like to ride a motorcycle now that I bounce instead of crash. Do I have your permission?

Love, Hilee

Dear Hilee,

Now that you're dead, please, try anything you've ever wanted to experiment with. What can go wrong?

I'm so glad you can read again.

Sending love, Mom

February, Hilee's March Birthday Looms Like a Belligerent Ghost

The specter of my daughter's upcoming March 5th birthday haunts me, darkening my days. In past years, I also celebrated Hilee's birthday as my Anniversary of Being a Mother.

Without Hilee, the anniversary is hollow. During this time, I miss her terribly. Although ironically, because of our correspondence, on her birthday I spend more time with her in spirit than I often got to spend in person.

Dear Hilee,

I've been thinking about your upcoming birthday. I want to mark the day, but I'm not sure how. Any ideas?

Love, Mom

Dear Mom,

Do you think I will actually be a year older on March 5 or am I always going to be 47?

Definitely, you should mark the moment. After all, it's your anniversary of becoming a mom as well as my birthday. You and Ron should at least get your traditional Cascone's meals.

I wonder if they ever give you a hall pass here? In the movies, dead people sometimes return home for special occasions.

If this were real life, I'd be asking, "What are you going to give me for my birthday?" If I were still alive, what would you get me?

Curious, Hilee

Dear Hilee,

If you were still alive, I'd be singing the *Hallelujah Chorus*! But wait, no I wouldn't, because that would drive you crazy. What would you like? I haven't spent any money on you for months—that does not feel right!

Love, Mom

Dear Mom,

Normally, I'd want money, even though there's nothing here to buy. Still, inquiring minds want to know—how much would you give me? Last year, it was $50. Plus, a good birthday meal at the restaurant of my choice. Or was it $75? Since I am getting so close to age 50, I would lobby for $100. Deal?   Love, Hilee

Dear Hilee,

Deal. Can you come to collect your prize?

Love, Mom

Dear Mom,

Hahaha! I don't think so.

Love, Hilee, Stuck in Space

Dear Mom,

I don't want you to die, but I wish you could come for a visit. All my secrecy and shame are pretty much gone. I'm not mad at myself anymore, even though I fucked up a lot. I'm feeling more "cosmic" and "in the flow" than I did on Earth. Wasn't that one of your dreams for me? Are we worried I'm going to lose my personality and turn into a gooey marshmallow?

Get out the hot chocolate, just in case.

Love, H

Dear Hilee,

I go for my yearly mammogram. Though I've healed from my long-ago breast cancer, I still dread this test and its results. Fear and trembling are my companions as I take off my shirt and don the open pink hospital gown with the mysterious ties that don't meet in the middle or the top or the bottom. I have to fold my arms across my chest to stay covered.

The pain of each x-ray makes me light-headed. Between the crushing tests of my breasts, I drink water and take deep breaths. To distract myself, I ask my technician about her hobbies and family. She eagerly describes her two teenage daughters. Then, as she is draping my arm over the machine, positioning me, she says, "Do you have children?"

I stare ahead, mind buzzing. If I simply say I have two daughters, will she ask me questions that I won't want to answer? If I tell her I have two daughters and one of them is dead, will she look so stricken that I'll feel guilty at imposing my grief on her?

"I have one daughter and two grandchildren," I say, wanting our easy conversation to continue. Instantly, bile burns in my throat. I have denied you, dear Hilee, something I vowed never to do. I have desecrated my role as your mother. I have lied about one of the largest truths in my life.

When the mammogram is complete and I am dressed again, I trudge to my car, heavy with my betrayal.

This is my confession, Hilee. And I hope you will forgive me. I believe you will, because you are beyond all this now. But I am not. I am in the muddy, messy middle and I realize anew how essential you are—living or dead—to me and to my well-being.

Love, Mom

Dear Mom,

A woman cannot be held accountable for what she blurts out during the tortuous tactics of the mammo-monster. You are forgiven.

Hilee-gram

Dear Hilee,

I went to a grief group via Zoom. The people were strong, welcoming, and had each been through so much. Listening to their stories, I felt lucky you lived so long. One woman's son died at age 21 and another woman's daughter died at age 33. I'm grateful you weren't doing hard drugs until later in life. Although, if you were alive, I might ask, "Why did you start?" I thought you were moving into a more contented space. Of course, if you were still alive, I wouldn't know you were taking drugs!

Love, Mom

Dear Mom,

Can you imagine how worried you'd have been if you knew I was doing drugs? You'd be trying everything to get me to stop.

Mom, the drugs put me into such a different space, introduced me to a whole new group of people, blasted open my mind, like I was zipping into the cosmos. I didn't think about how dangerous it was. But I'm not sure I would have stopped even if someone had explained the perils. I probably would have thought, *That happens to other people, not me.*

Up here, I keep meaning to look around for a woman friend, but time slips by like a raft on a river (Hmmm, I like that) and I forget. But now, I'm remembering: always good to have a woman friend.

Love, H

Dear Hilee,

If you were alive, you'd be calling and texting me about the upcoming winter storm and asking me to get you chocolate and Diet Coke, so you wouldn't suffer if you were snowed in. You were a great weather girl. Plus, you always gave me permission not to drive if ice or snow were on the streets! Now I have to turn on the local news—not nearly as interesting.

Love, Mom

Dear Mom,

That was a special service, just for you and sometimes for Sarah. Dad never cared about weather—the more terrifying the storm, the more he loved to barrel through it in his SUV.

Love, Hilee the Omniscient

Dear Mom,

Did you know there are no real rooms here? No walls, no doors, no windows. I just have to whisper, "I need some privacy," and suddenly I can't see anyone—and when I say anyone, I mean shadowy figures, floating wraiths, spectral ghostlike images, not full-bodied people. Also, they can't see me. At least I think they can't see me. But here, no one is looking at anyone else. Mainly because we all look sort of the same. Except for our clothes.

Love, Hilee

Dear Hilee,

Have you come across any potential female friends?

Love, Mom

Dear Mom,

Back home, people fell into my life. An acquaintance had a chum who was down on her luck and needed a sofa to sleep on for a few nights. I always invited that person/persons over. And most of the time, we became friends.

Here, if I want to meet someone, I have to wander around. Probably I'll get lost, since there are no streets or road signs. Maybe I don't have to return to this spot; I can hang out anywhere.

You know how Apple always saves data in the cloud? Clouds are everywhere and I don't see a bunch of data poking through any of them. Makes you wonder.

Love, H, Temporarily Stored in the Clouds.

Dear Hilee,

Happy Larry's Birthday! If you were here, you'd be missing your dad. You and I often talked about what an enigmatic person he was—a mixture of magic, manipulation, loyalty, fierceness, bullshit, intellect, ego, anger, creativity, entrepreneurship, survival skills, and random caring. You have his intellect, fierceness, loyalty, and magic, with a dash of ego and anger thrown in.

Anyhow, I am guessing you're thinking about Larry Robert Shouse, born February 3, 1947. Me too.

Love, Mom

Dear Mom,

Only a dash of ego and anger? Come on, Mom, you know I have plenty of those. I was thinking about chicken-fried steak, which Dad really liked. He adored all those fatty southern foods. I was trying to remember if he ever cooked for us. Grilling, I'm sure. Black-eyed peas on New Year's Day. Chili, shrimp. Remember when he got angry and threw a whole sizzling pan of bacon into the backyard, because you'd burned a piece?

Love, H

Dear Hilee,

It is hard to forget a large angry man charging through a suburban kitchen, seizing a greasy pan of frying bacon, opening up the sliding doors to the deck, and tossing pan and pork into the back yard.

Back then, I was a co-dependent, struggling mother married to an addictive, explosive, mentally unbalanced man. I was ardently trying to keep our family together. I never threw anything. Mainly because I didn't want to have to clean it up later.

Love, Mom

Dear Mom,

That's your problem: too responsible. I've thrown stuff and let it stay on the floor. When you're really mad and self-righteous, you don't even think about the mess.

I used to be so angry at life and people. But now, I'm like a stick of melting butter. Is this my forever? Or is there even such a thing as forever?

Love, H

Dear Hilee,

As best I can tell, "forever" keeps changing. I thought you'd be with me "forever," at least as long as I was alive.

A friend's daughter just killed herself. I am so sad about this, not only for her and for her family, but for myself. All those feelings, the phone call in the night, the news of your death, my unfathomable grief, flood me again. Thank goodness we're writing to each other, since we can't talk on the phone anymore.

Can you tell I miss you?

Love, Mom

Dear Mom,

Suicide isn't as easy as it sounds. You need nerves of steel. So often I felt totally despairing. But never quite enough to kill myself. I guess I was lazy. Or lucky. Or maybe you were the lucky ones.

Love, H

Dear Hilee,

So many times, I worried about you taking your own life. You often announced: "I feel like killing myself."

Those words curdled my heart. Remember how irritated you were when I asked if you "had a suicide plan?" My therapist taught me that. I hated saying it.

Instead, I felt like begging, "Please, please, please, don't kill yourself."

But maybe my therapist was right, because you did not do yourself in. Intentionally, that is. Having a script of things to say when you threatened suicide helped me act calm and not beg. Perhaps it also helped me be less afraid.

Still, when you were angry at me and went silent for days on end, I worried myself into knots, frightened you would hurt yourself and die. I'm grateful you lived so long.

Love, Mom

Dear Mom,

I never thought I'd be as old as 40, let alone 47!

I miss bad dogs. Dogs who run away just for the adventure of it. Dogs who chew up your favorite tennis shoes, put their paws on the kitchen counter, and devour the leftover roast beef you were saving for dinner. Mutts who wag their tail and lick you when you scold, "Bad dog! Bad dog!" I miss my Muddy!

Love, H

Dear Mom,

All the feelings that ripped through me on Earth, random ups and downs and sideways emotions zapping me, trapping me, confusing me, engrossing me, flattening me, exhausting me—all are gone. I am blank.

The floating guides might say, "You are peaceful."

Peaceful means I've lost my mojo. But that mojo was probably just anger, despair, and a desire for revenge. Plus, my addiction to stirring things up to see how far I could go.

Would you like me in this calm state? Probably you'd miss the old irascible me? (How do you like that word—irascible? First time I've used it in a sentence.)

Love, Hilee, Goddess of Words

Dear Hilee,

I'm impressed with your use of "irascible!" (First time I've used it in a sentence.) I would like to experience the calm you.

I agree, being calm can seem boring. But I'm glad your emotions are more merry-go-round and less roller coaster.

Love, Mother of the Word-Goddess

Dear Mom,

When the guides sense an upset, they pause and hover, which bothers me. Who are these creatures? Is being a guide a reward or a punishment? And why would I want someone around when I'm anxious? Yes, I still feel anxious because I don't know what I'm supposed to be doing. I don't know the rules.

They say, "Be who you are. You are perfect the way you are." This is supposed to be comforting? I am confused about who I am!

I've gained a whole new wardrobe but lost myself. What is the point of new clothes without SnapChat photos and someone to share them with!

Anyhow, would you like to hear what I'm wearing? A slinky teal blue tank top with sparkles, a fitted forest green velvet jacket and tight ripped jeans. Matthew would go crazy over this outfit. Lothar probably won't notice.

Where are all the females? Too bad they didn't just plop me in a dorm so I'd be around women. But probably that would drive me batty—too much noise and bitchiness. Okay, I've made a decision. I'm going to read page 1of the manual and then walk around. I'm not in the mood to watch a video.

Hilee, the Bold Explorer

Dear Bold Explorer,

Oh, brave new world. Hooray for reading page 1 and looking around.

Love, Mom

Dear Mom,

After all my anxiety about opening the manual, page 1 is almost blank. It says, OPEN UP.

What the heck does that mean? I thought I would read the rules, get some tips on how to fly and how to acquire a cell phone that beams back to Kansas, Dorothy. Well, I guess if a place has permission to be mysterious, ambiguous, and woo-woo, it's the after-life.

Now for page 2 of the story—I'm going out. Probably to The Edge of Convenience, looking for Lothar and some forbidden Diet Coke.

Love, H

Dear Hilee,

Naturally, I like the advice on page 1. And, you're already doing it.

In life, you had to hide so much, covering up your tender sweetness and your deep longing and sadness with prickly irritation, rage, and fear. What if you allow yourself to just be? Maybe you can become a floating guide. Oh wait, that sounds like me asking you to finish college. I take it back!

I'll be talking to my therapist today. Anything special you'd like me to ask?

Love, Mom

Dear Mom,

How many times are you going to talk to that therapist? Is it all about me?

I'd like you to ask her: How the fuck am I supposed to be myself? I honestly do not know what that means. And particularly now that I'm having this bizarre out-of-body-experience. Remember that children's story about the goose whose golden coins were stolen? The goose waddled around chanting, "Click, click, clack. I want my money back." Well, I want my body back. Except for my teeth. My terrible, rotting, teeth. I'd like new ones, please.

Love, Hilee

Dear Hilee,

I remember that story. Also, "Never tease a weasel, Not even once or twice, The weasel will not like it, And teasing isn't nice!" Words to live by, indeed.

The therapy is all about me. But I'll ask your question.

Love, Mom

Dear Hilee,

Did you go on your expedition?

I did ask Eve your question, "How the fuck am I supposed to be myself?"

She said, "How do you, Hilee, define yourself?"

Then she read me a quote, "Stop trying to define yourself."

Love, Mom

Dear Mom,

"How do I define myself?" That sounds just like a therapist, throwing out an impossible question instead of giving a straight answer. If I knew who I was, well....maybe I do know. When I was alive, I considered myself a fuck-up and a disappointment. Occasionally, I thought I was nice and caring, particularly when I was helping someone. With certain people, I was sexy and intense. Now I have no idea who I am because there's no drama or desire or family to bounce off of.

Love, H

Dear Hilee,

Last night Sarah texted a link to a newspaper article from January 13, "Woman serving 30-day sentence dies of apparent suicide in Clay County jail."

Hilee, that woman was Candi, your former housemate!

I could not believe that she killed herself in jail. They are "investigating" and gave no details. They were scheduled to release her days earlier but had detained her because of a possible felony charge. She was listed as homeless, with her last address in Overland Park, Kansas, I'm guessing at your house.

I looked up her obituary and she was cremated at

the Barnett Family Funeral Home in Oskaloosa, Kansas. A funeral home in rural Kansas bearing my maiden name! When I read that, I went to bed and pulled the covers over my head. The Universe is messing with us. And it's not a beautiful mess.

I wanted you to know, if you didn't already.

With love and sorrow, Mom

Dear Mom,

Oh my God. I can't believe it. Candi, homeless. Dead in a jail cell. She used to have a job and was a semi-normal person, albeit one with anger issues and a compulsion to manipulate and intimidate.

That news really knocks me out.

I loved Candi, but she was toxic. She bossed me around in my own house, belittling me and making me feel worthless. As if I couldn't feel rotten on my own. She stopped paying rent and ate all of my food, without ever replacing it. I couldn't stand to leave my room when she was there.

I finally kicked her out and later, I felt so strong and brave when I didn't let her move back in. You were very proud that I stood up for myself.

But what if I had let her move back in? Would she still be alive? Would I still be alive? Probably we'd both have made each other miserable, then died anyway. Right?

I'm lying down and putting my blankets over my head.

Love, Hilee

Dear Hilee,

You were so scared and unhappy living with her. You absolutely did the right thing, keeping her out of your house. Still, it's sad, sad, sad.

Love, Mom

Dear Mom,

I finally went on my expedition, dressed in a green velvet jacket and slithery camouflage leggings. I looked great, for a dead person. Lothar appeared—maybe I conjured him up—and we chatted. He's not working on himself either.

"I'm fine the way I am," he said. Anyway, talk about Lucy in the Skies with Diamonds, he had a joint to share. I asked if he knew where the women lived, and he shrugged. He said, "What manual? Are these dinosaurs still printing out instructions?"

He and Dad could be friends: he's a rabid Libertarian. Not me. I'm more of a random rebel. I like to know what the rules are, even if I don't want to follow them.

Love, Hilee

Dear Hilee,

Lothar sounds interesting. Maybe page 2 will tell you how to find the women. Or maybe all you have to do is wish for a friend and she will appear. Have you tried it?

Love, Mom

Dear Mom,

Today I am wearing a tuxedo and top hat, with a starched white shirt: the Fred-Astaire-tap dancing-with-Ginger-Rogers look.

Did I tell you I haven't noticed anyone smoking regular cigarettes? I'm sure there's some "tobacco pipeline." Isn't there a saying, "Where there's people, there's smoke"?

I know you were upset that I smoked. I know you worried I'd get lung cancer and die a painful early death. But guess what—it didn't make any difference.

Still, you were sweet to worry. It showed you loved me and wanted me to live a long time. And probably, you didn't want me to become a miserable, hacking, I-can't-breathe invalid that you had to take care of.

Love, H

Dear Hilee,

I wish you could drop by on March 5th, OUR holiday, your date of birth, and my anniversary of being a mother. Whatever am I going to do?

Meanwhile, this is a perfect time to be gloomy and indoors. The wind is blowing, the sleet is snowing.

If you want to smoke, I won't pester you about it!

Love, Mom

Dear Mom,

Page 2 of the manual says, TAKE A STEP. The writer was definitely not getting paid by the word. I went ahead and took a step. Nothing happened. I'm considering taking another one soon. Ha ha ha!

I like smoking and I like the challenge of figuring out where the tobacco is. I may go to The Edge and see if anyone's around. Or maybe I'll take a few extra steps and find a new corner. Maybe I'll take so many steps, I'll become a sports hero.

Remember when I won an orange ribbon on Field Day? Although they probably gave everyone a ribbon.

Today I am wearing dungarees (isn't that a great word!), a black tank top and a worn black leather jacket, with lots of Harley and Sturgis patches on it. Oh, and combat boots. Anybody attracted by this outfit will surely have a cigarette.

Love, H

Dear Hilee,

I'm impressed you've already taken so many

steps! Who knows where those will lead you.

I wish you could meet Juno and Coco, our guinea pigs. Once you banished your prejudice against rodents, you would like them. They love to tunnel and hide. They're peaceful animals, sitting around and eating hay. When they're out of hay, Juno wheeks (a squeaky noise they use to communicate with humans) to let me know. Coco doesn't speak much—she just puts her feet on her hay dish and looks soulfully at me. They were a big help during the isolation of the pandemic and now that you're dead, they're even more important. Is it embarrassing to confess that my emotional support animal is a guinea pig?

I will be having no adventures today, so I look forward to hearing yours.

Love, Mom

Dear Hilee,

Exactly seven months ago, I received the late-night call from Matthew, shouting into the phone that something was wrong, that you weren't breathing. Just writing those words turns my whole body to concrete. The sadness over your death amplifies my emotions and makes me feel hopeless, left out, and upset over every little thing. I am usually quite good at counting my blessings, but when I think about you being dead, I forget how to count.

You and I have changed places: I'm sad and depressed and you're upbeat and hopeful. Any advice?

Love, Mom

Dear Mom,

Ha! That's a good one. Me give you advice on being upbeat. But you're right, maybe depression is only for the living. Once you're dead, all those things that were so important—who loves me, do they love me enough, how am I going to get to the grocery store, what can I do for fun, how can I pay the vet bill if my dog gets sick?—all those troubles are gone.

But Mom, you're still in the thick of things and me dying hasn't helped. I always thought you'd be happier if I weren't around. Guess I was wrong. Maybe you liked worrying about me?

As for advice, even though I'm not depressed, I have some of the feelings that used to flatten me. Only now, they don't bother me. When I was lying in my bed in my messy clothes-strewn bedroom on Grandview Lane, the thought, *Nothing matters*, was a hippo squatting on my chest, immobilizing me, squashing motivation and hope.

But now the idea that "nothing matters" is a relief. I can "breathe" again, which is rather ironic.

What if you took the feelings that dragged you

through mud and cow dung and said, "Nothing matters. Hilee's dead and it doesn't matter."

Then, and here I'm channeling you, I recommend "making a list of all the good things in your life." Hmmm, maybe I was actually listening to your self-help advice.

Ha ha ha.

Let me know what you think. And later, I'll tell you how I got my smokes.

Teaser: The Doctor Was In, Now the doctor is going out to see her new friend!

Hilee, therapist-at-large

Dear Hilee,

New friend! Smokes! Tell me more.

Meanwhile, I'm glad you were listening when I was desperate to help you. I so wanted you to be happier, dear Hilee. Well, now you are. So, when people pat my hand and say, "She's in a better place now," maybe they're right. You do seem like you're in a better place.

Love, Mom

Dear Mom,

Wearing my biker clothes, I step outside my bubble. And instantly smell cigarette smoke. I follow the heavenly aroma. (That could be a pun, depending on

72

if I'm really in heaven! But I don't think I am, because aren't all your dead friends and relatives supposed to joyously greet you?)

A mountain of a woman stands in my path. It's not a real path, but it's the general area of my next step. She grips a skinny home-made (or heaven-made) ciggie. It's so delicious-looking I almost drool. But I'm not sure you can actually drool here. The woman's wearing a white undershirt and ultra-tight worn-out jeans. Her arms and shoulders crawl with tattoos! I blurt, "How did you get those tattoos!?"

She laughs and passes me the smoke. Imagine you haven't tasted chocolate in seven months, and someone gives you a Milky Way Midnight candy bar. Multiply that ecstasy by 20 and you'll understand that I want to kiss that wreckage of paper and tobacco and whisper, "You complete me!"

But somehow your voice appears in my head, intoning, *Share*. So I take only one draw. Then she says, "I manifested these tattoos."

Which is amazing, because (and don't be grossed out by this) we don't really have skin here, except on our faces. So she's actually managed to manifest skin and tattoos! She's illustrated her whole life—motorcycle, VW van, beer bottles, a German shepherd—in bright, eye-popping colors that would have cost a fortune on Earth.

"How did you do it?" I ask.

"I took a meditation class when I was in prison and learned to focus on what I wanted. It works way quicker up here than it did when I was alive."

Good news: she's going to teach me. Mom, I'm actually going to start meditating. Bet you never saw that coming.

If I had my phone, I'd send you a picture of the two of us! Her name used to be Karen, but she changed it to Rock.

I'm learning to meditate and you're learning that nothing really matters. What a deal.

Love, H

Dear Mom,

Rock is amazing. You'd think, by the way she looks, she'd be all gruff and impatient. That prison meditation must have worked some magic: she's calm. We went to The Edge and sat on the mythical curb and counted our breaths. It was surprisingly exhilarating.

Feel free to say, "I told you so," because…it doesn't matter!

After we meditated, Rock told me about her life, and I told her about mine.

Hers was way more interesting. She says, "I was a wrestler, a waitress, a wife, and a wobber."

"What's a wobber?"

"Have you heard of Elmer Fudd?"

Then I burst out laughing because I got it: a robber. All her other careers started with Ws.

Anyhow, the Elmer Fudd capers put her into prison. After her third marriage went bust, she gathered together some "women friends." Her friends were not like yours: they were feminist, Robin Hood meth addicts. They robbed men who were selling drugs at big margins and re-sold the stuff at fair prices.

"Once I gave up trying to be married, I started having more fun," Rock told me. "I wish I'd figured it out sooner: I might still be alive. But then I wouldn't have all these dope tattoos."

I know, it's weird when an addict says "dope" about skin ink.

So, Mom, you are probably the only woman in your zip code with a dead daughter who's learning to meditate so she can manifest tattoos. Congratulations!

Love, Hilee, the semi-blank canvas

Dear Hilee,

I am indeed proud you're meditating. I am wondering, "Who shall I brag to first?" Probably Ron. He's the original Breathe-in, Breathe-out proponent and he's been to many workshops all about deepening and controlling the breath. So, he will be thrilled with your news.

Rock sounds interesting. Have you considered what kinds of tattoos you want?

I am "breathlessly" awaiting the next installment of Hilee and her meditation guru.

Love, Mom

Dear Mom,

Those deep breaths must be working. Or maybe it was having a new friend. I felt so brave that I opened the manual to page 3. Guess what it said?

COME IN.

Are these people trying to save on ink?

I wish they'd make a bullet list and stop tiptoeing around. Isn't being dead about bare bones and honesty? I am not going to ponder these two words: I'm just going to breathe, counting one, two, three, four in and hold two, three, four, and out two three four. But don't worry: I'm only doing that so Rock will like me. Otherwise, it's too boring.

What if the manual had instructed, "Come Inhale?" Then I might have gotten chills.

Love, Hilee

Dear Hilee,

Speaking of chills, I've been thinking about your favorite *Guys and Dolls* tune today: *Miss Adelaide's La-*

ment, hearing Adelaide warbling "A person could develop a cold" in her thick East Coast accent. I am such a person and I have a cold today. At first, I thought, *Oh no!* Then, because of your advice that nothing matters, I thought, *Oh yes*. I have an excuse not to be on top of things today.

I am intrigued by the manual's "Come in."

So many interesting phrases include those two innocent words.

Come in to my parlor.

Little pig, little pig, let me come in.

Her ship has come in.

She has come in second.

And an all-time favorite, straight from the musical *Chicago*, "She had it come-in."

But when I think about you right now, I see you "Come In to your own true self."

Talk about taking a big step!

Love, Mom

Dear Hilee,

Today we had a consult with the behavior team at the Down Syndrome Guild, to learn more ways to work with your fascinating niece, our amazing granddaughter, Annabelle.

We asked, "What do we do when Annabelle tells a lie?"

The behaviorist said, "She's lying? That's fabulous news: Lying is a significant cognitive development."

The whole team of specialists applauded. Ron and I looked at each other. Instead of worrying that our granddaughter was breaking a commandment, we beamed because of her advanced reasoning.

"It takes a lot of skill to figure out what is truth, what people want to hear, and what is a good lie," the behaviorist told us.

I've always thought lying was a sin, but now I know it's also an accomplishment!

Love, Mom

Dear Hilee,

Remember when you had a psychotic breakdown and you completely melted down in your driveway? Carlton had to call an ambulance to rush you to the hospital. Once there, you lied to the psychiatrist about taking drugs. But they'd drawn blood when you were admitted and unusual illegal substances turned up in your system.

That was a horrible day. Carlton called and said you were in the ER. Ron and I hurried to the hospital, terrified. You must have been plenty scared too.

Love, Mom

Dear Mom,

I'm glad to know lying is an advanced cognitive skill. I never really used that skill much. Although I lied to you about smoking, and certainly drugs. Why upset you with the truth?

I hope you're not thinking, *If only I'd known Hilee was doing drugs, maybe she'd still be alive.*

You would've been worrying and lecturing me, and it wouldn't have changed a thing.

I like your "come in" list. Isn't there a bunch of Bible stuff about "come in all you faithful" or is that just a Christmas carol?

Did you follow my "Nothing matters" advice? Or are you like me and haven't gotten around to it yet? Come on in, and fess up.

Love, H

Dear Hilee,

I confess, I haven't yet done it. But I'm going to make my list. Soon. Maybe on my favorite holiday, March 4th, the only day of the year that commands you to move forward. Maybe.

Sending love, Mom

Dear Hilee,

Your cousin Zach sent us a gorgeous picture: he and his beloved fiancé Brian are holding their fluffy white dogs in front of the weeping willow tree they planted in your memory on their land in upstate New York.

Zach said, "It was a cold, gray, cloudy day. Just as Brian and I reached Hilee's tree, a shaft of sunlight illuminated it, so she was glowing gold."

They picked out such a fabulous tree for you. Even in the winter, without its leaves, it looks beautiful and mighty. Their friend, a landscape architect, said the tree was planted in a perfect place.

So, you are now planted in a perfect place. And you are branching out.

Love, Mom

Dear Hilee,

Here are some things that bother me:

~ Knowing you are dead.

~ Feeling left out, unloved, ignored. This is from childhood, being a dorky-looking Jewish girl wearing over-sized hand-me-down clothes in the very evangelical Christian South.

~ Worrying that people I love are not taking care of themselves or are unhappy—the Jewish mother thing again. I so want to help them! As my psychologist friend used to say when I'd call him during your teen years because I was worried about you, "Deborah, is this your business?" I secretly thought it was, but he expertly explained it was not.

Guess what, Hilee? I tried your advice: I took my list and paired it with "Nothing matters!" Then I said, "Ha ha ha." Doing that actually boosted my spirits. Not that it matters.

What other advice do you have for me?

Love, Mom

Dear Mom,

I am impressed. First, that you followed my advice and then that it actually worked. It makes me want to try it out on someone else. But who?

I've been pondering my potential tattoos. The sky is literally the limit here. I don't have to worry about inappropriate art on my arms and not being able to get a job. I wasn't even worried about that on Earth because I never really wanted to work. Plus, for so many years I was so depressed, so medicated I didn't want to do anything, except drink Diet cokes and eat chocolate.

I guess that was hard on you. I never thought about it at the time; it was just the way things were. Dad would tell me I was useless, and I figured he was right. But probably, he wasn't.

Remember when you told me I had a gift for drawing? I didn't believe you, but now I'm drawing pictures of potential tattoos and they're good. I'm designing clothes and the clothes are cute.

I drew this amazing zombie tattoo, but I'm not sure I should get it. Zombies are the scary undead and as far as I know, I am the un-scary dead. Zombies are bloodied and stiff, stinking of rotting flesh. I am floating around in a cotton candy bubble. It would be fun if I were a bit more scary. Perhaps I should contact hair and make-up and see what they can do!

Love, H

Dear Hilee,

How about a tattoo with an old-fashioned heart pierced by an arrow, with the word *Mother* at its center? Sarah might suggest one with the word *Sister*.

Love, Mom

Dear Mom,

Just like one of the World War I Navy tattoos, huh? Blue-black ink, crudely done? It's a kitsch idea and I'll think about it. Rock might laugh herself silly when I tell her. I'm hoping to bounce into her today for another breathe-in lesson.

Love, Hilee

Dear Mom,

Rock loved your idea of the old-fashioned Mother/Sister tattoos. She thought it was genius. She's thinking of getting one that says Mr. Vroom, the name of her motorcycle. (She never cared much for her mother.)

I asked if she'd read the manual and she said, "What manual? I figured out everything for myself my whole damned life. I never asked for help."

"Why didn't you ask for help?"

I always, always asked for help, even when I didn't need it. I wanted to make sure that you or Sarah or Dad really loved me and that was one way I could find out.

"Never thought I'd get it." she said. "Don't like to be rejected."

You can see, Rock and I are totally different, yet we are sitting on The Edge, breathing in together. Trying to manifest! Who would have thought!

Love, Hilee the Mystic

Dear Mystical Daughter,

During your life, you were excellent at manifesting. You'd be worried about food or money or… Someone would come along with just what you needed. I often marveled at how gifts flowed into your life at exactly the right moment. So, I believe this intentional manifestation will be a huge success. While you're up there, you might consider taking flying lessons.

Love, Mom

Dear Mom,

Flying lessons is a fabulous idea. I'll ask one of the floating guides, although their answers are usually too cryptic to understand.

Love, H

Dear Hilee,

Tonight I feel incredibly sorrowful. I went on a walk and somehow you came with me. I thought of all the times you and I did not understand each other. You could not grasp the depth and nature of my love and I could not absorb the heaviness and pervasiveness of your mental illnesses. It was difficult for me to appreciate you and now it is wrenching to be without you.

Even when I wasn't your ideal mother and you weren't my ideal daughter, I always hoped we'd come closer, and deepen our relationship. This letter writing is connecting us. But it would be much, much better if I could see you.

I feel lucky you and I spent time together the last week of your life, when you were happy. Of course, maybe you were happy because of drugs.

Love, Mom

Dear Mom,

Mom, I did appreciate you, in my way. You were an amazingly nice person. You were heroic for not giving up on me and trying to help me, even though I was irritated by your persistent desire to change me.

Some of my friends didn't even speak to their parents, things were so bad between them. Things never got that bad for you and me. You never yelled at me or called me names. You always fought fair, when I could get you to fight. Remember when I encouraged you to yell and curse and argue and finally, you did? It was fun, right? You felt great, right?

I liked how you wrote essays about our everyday growing up life. When I read those stories, I realized how much you loved me. But I couldn't remember your love when I felt depressed or unhappy.

I also appreciated you taking me to Sprouts every month. Knowing you would buy me fruits and vegetables was comforting. And the way you introduced me to Ron's cousin Janet after Dad's memorial service was one of the best things ever.

Too bad I didn't make this list of appreciations when I was alive. But I did email several days before I died, thanking you. I wasn't planning on dying when I wrote that, in case you were wondering.

Love, H

Dear Hilee,

I did wonder. But I figured you were not suicidal, so I decided not to dwell on that. I feel so lucky we can send each other these letters now. I guess it's true: never too late.

Now, we need something fun to talk about.

I was proud of your ability to learn and speak Spanish. Your adventurousness in going to Costa Rica and staying with a family. You could cook. Your great memory, recalling in detail movies, books, music.

Here's something about our guinea pigs. They like to rest when nothing is going on. They are peaceful, until I come along and offer them extra hay. When I stop typing or I stand, Juno looks up with a hopeful expression, wanting either hay, pets, or playtime. I am always ready to pet her.

Now, they are each resting in their habitat and their presence is calming. Every evening, each of them jumps into a green "cuddle cave." I pet Juno, and Ron pets Coco. Juno looks me in the eyes most of the time and I believe she's my little soul sister.

Love, Mom

Dear Hilee,

You can probably tell how much I am missing you. Maybe instead of learning to fly, someone will sprinkle pixie dust and allow you to soar.   Love, Mom

Dear Mom,

Homonyms are so interesting. Soar and Sore, for example. If the pixie dust works, I will soar. If it fails, I will be sore from the crash. I am always indebted to root words.

Rock says I need to draw my new tattoos before I can manifest them. Otherwise, something hinky might emerge. Yes, she said "hinky." I have no idea where that word came from.

So, for my right shoulder, my heart with an arrow and *Mother*. For my left shoulder, in honor of Sarah, a heart with an arrow and *Sister*. I am thinking of a giant dog somewhere, in honor of Muddy and Vesta. Then a quote or two, but nothing too dark, like I would normally want if I were alive. But I don't want anything too inspiring, which I might want if I were enlightened.

Wouldn't it be weird if I were enlightened before you and Ron? That would be tragically unfair and absolutely hysterical!

Love, Hilee

March, the Month of My Daughter's Birth

T. S. Eliot wrote, "April is the cruelest month." But this year, for me, it's March. Taunting me, staring through me, pumping me with dread.

I wake up on March 5th, which is my "anniversary of being a mom." I am short of breath, long on sorrow, because my anniversary child is no longer alive. In our correspondence, Hilee says, "There's only one letter between OM and MOM." She hints that she is meditating. Stranger things have happened, but really, I can't think what.

Dear Hilee,

Less than a week before your birthday. If you were here, you might be in bed all this week, depressed about your advanced age. Or you might let people take you out for pre-birthday celebrations. We would have already discussed several times what gifts you wanted, probably a combination of money and frothy clothing from Etsy. Forty-eight, Hilee. My 48th anniversary of being a mom. Mind-boggling!

I am going to ask Ron to sprinkle some of your

ashes in Cascone's bushes. My plan for your ash-sprin-
kling focuses on restaurants you like: Sonic, of course,
Bo Ling's, Taco Bell, Thai Place, the Quik Trip near
your house. Maybe a pizza place? I envision a sacred
progressive dinner, without the food. But I haven't
been able to do that yet. Too final. Too emotional.

I am determined to have a better day than yesterday, even if part of it is finishing taxes and washing the
guinea pigs' tunnels.

Love, Mom

Dear Mom,

I would definitely be in bed this week, freaked out
over being almost fifty! True, just weeks before I died,
I decided I wanted to live, to see what could happen
between me and Matthew. Instead, I'm here with softy
blankies, fake but cuddly dogs, pablum TV, and great
art supplies.

Did I tell you I met a man with a pair of binoculars?
It's amazing what happens when you leave your bubble.

Yesterday, in a burst of *je-ne-sais-quoi*, (ha ha ha) I
decided to go outside. I wondered, if I bounced high
enough, could I flap my arms and fly like Peter Pan?
So, I bounced and actually went up a little. That scared
me. I thought I was going to zoom off into space, so I
shouted, "Help!"

Then I heard, "Shhhh." Nearby stood a being wearing cargo pants, a vest with pockets, a T-Shirt that said, "I love to watch." (Kind of creepy, huh?) He was peering through the substantial pair of binoculars around his neck.

He said, "You are disturbing me." He might have been full of needle punctures down his arms if we'd met while alive.

"What are you doing?" I asked.

"Studying life on the home planet."

"Why?"

"Someday we will be leaving this place and I want to be prepared. I want to do a better job of staying away from the law."

That got my attention: a guy who doesn't want to be a more upright citizen, just doesn't want to get caught. So, we started talking.

"Can you see anything?" I asked.

"Actually, I can see perfectly without the spyglasses. I just like the look. Reminds of me of my halcyon days with the mortals."

Who uses *halcyon*? I've always enjoyed a robust vocabulary. Mom, this guy, Arvin, was a birdwatcher and a thief. He had a photographic memory and would join all these birding clubs, pretending he was an ornithologist. He'd make friends, then when he'd visit people's homes, he'd steal something, usually money or jewelry.

Later, I'm going to find out how he did it. But don't worry: I won't become a thief. Too much work making friends with all those strangers.

So, now besides Santa and me, Arvin's watching you.

Love, H

Dear Hilee,

Arvin sounds like quite a character. What if he's right? What if you do eventually come back to Earth? Can we arrange for a secret meeting? A passcode so that even if we don't recognize each other, we'll know each other? Or maybe you'll start all over and arrive as a baby. What kind of family do you want this time? A sunshiny family or a dodgier group of relations?

I always thought I'd have a normal, happy family, but once you marry an addictive, narcissistic person, those chances diminish. Maybe it's better to have an interesting family, though even the most normal-seeming people have their hidden darkness.

Love, Mom

Dear Mom,

Gosh, Mom, you sound like someone who needs to get outside and take a walk. All this talk of sunshine and family. I guess you've already forgotten my amazing cosmic wisdom: "Nothing matters. Ha ha ha."

The Doctor Is In, But Is Going Out To Watch

Dear Mom,

Arvin is a font of information. Evidently there's a group of souls who do not want to return to Earth. Arvin has infiltrated them, even though there's nothing to steal because no one has anything.

"I can steal their secrets," he says. This is what it has come to.

They believe the planet is destined to die soon, and they don't want to be part of that. Plus, they're comfortable here. I'd like to meet these folks, because I'm betting they're misfits, like me. Maybe I'd like to stay here too, although it is rather dull. Still, surprisingly, I'm not going out of my mind with boredom. Yet. Although I wouldn't mind getting into a good righteous argument with someone.

Love, H

Dear Hilee,

Glad it's not me you want to argue with! I am a poor combatant. And you are an expert.

Well, it's a mere two days before your birthday and I am feeling sad, sad, sad. Yesterday we went to see the snow geese at Loess Bluffs. A million migrating birds passing through during hunting season. They had an idyllic frolic and feast at the lake. But afterward, if they flew in the wrong direction, they risked getting shot by hunters. We heard the guns from a not-too-distant field. All I could think about was dead birds. How can anyone know the right direction, the safe way, to fly or flee?

Love, Mom

Dear Hilee,

Today is March 4th, one of my favorite holidays. Did you know I am the "founder" of that holiday? At least a calendar blog once wrote that. I hope I don't succumb to Founder's Syndrome.

Forty-eight years ago on March 4th, with you swelling my belly, I went on a long, long walk. I got so tired I had to sit on the curb near 63rd and Troost to rest. Later that afternoon, a friend gave me a bumpy jeep ride, lurching over uneven terrain. I was trying to encourage you to come on out, to be born on March 4th, the only day of the year that tells you to move forward. But even then, you had your own ideas. The next night, after Larry had taken a sleeping pill and we'd gone to bed, I felt a wetness surrounding me. My gracious, had I peed in bed? Then I realized my water had broken.

I pried Larry from slumber and called my doctor.

We went to the hospital and hours later, you were born.

My only notion of childbirth was from reading *Gone With the Wind*, Melanie screaming how she was "torn asunder." I had a spinal injection, so I was not torn. But I was in awe the moment you arrived. You were a miracle and my real introduction to deep love.

Meanwhile, as founder of this prestigious holiday, I must ask, how are you going to March Forth today, my dear child?

Love, Mom

Dear Mom,

I wonder what it was like being a baby. We have that picture of me lying on Dad's chest and him just looking at me. You guys really loved me, didn't you?

I have a confession to make. I have been withholding information. Not lying, withholding. Withholding is a decision, not a sin.

Rock and I have been meditating every day. She calls it breathing manifestation, but I'm pretty darn sure it's every day Buddhist, hippie, yogi meditation. I didn't tell you because I didn't want you to worry I'm going over to the light side, that I'll become too woo woo for you!

Can you believe it? And what's even more disturbing—I like it. It's relaxing, soothing, just like you told me at least one hundred times. Too bad I didn't listen: I probably would have been less disturbed by everything.

Now, for another confession. (This is how I'm Marching Forth—confessing.) I'm not even sure I want tattoos anymore, which was the whole reason we were breathing and manifesting.

Today, I'm looking at the next page in the manual. Page 4 on March 4th. Pretty poetic, huh.

You know what they say, Mom, "There's no place like Om."

Love, H

Dear Hilee,

I'm so impressed with you and Rock and your breathing practices. Probably the meditation will show you how to fly.

I, too, have always wanted to fly. I used to dream about it all the time. It was never a blissful soaring on the air currents, like the hawks I so admire. I had to flap my arms to stay afloat. Still, it was worth it.

It sounds like you are practicing pages 1 and 2 of your manual: Open up. Take a step.

Love, Mom

Dear Hilee,

If you were here I'd be singing you the old Beatles

birthday song over the phone, "Na na na na na na, You say it's your birthday…" I'd be texting you, "Happy Birthday."

Matthew might have taken off work and the two of you would spend the day together. Or maybe Matthew would have had to work, and Ron and I would take you out to lunch.

Of course, you could be depressed and in bed with the covers over your head.

I will say it's gloomy having my *anniversary of being a mother* without you. Sure, it's still my anniversary, but you and I were the only ones who cared about that.

Yesterday I was thinking about all the things I learned from you. I remember standing in my garage back when we lived in Leawood. You were thirteen. We'd had a fight and I'd walked into the garage to gather calmness. A voice came into my head and said, "Hilee is your teacher." And it's true. Just by being yourself, you expanded my heart and my thinking. I was brought up to think people who carried too much body fat were undisciplined, lazy. You showed me differently, allowed me to see weight as protective body armor, as a way of healing from trauma. I was brought up to "get over" feelings of sadness and depression. You showed me that depression is a complicated mental illness. Your sudden fierceness and rage often scared me, and I had to learn to stop and ask myself, "Am I doing this for Hilee out of love or out of fear?"

"Everyone is on his or her own perfect path." This concept challenged me so many times and yet I believe it's true. You were on your perfect path, doing your best at all times. It was not my business to try to change you. As you read this, you may be thinking, "Really? I can't believe you stopped wanting to change me!"

You are right to be skeptical. But at least I toned myself down.

You showed me different ways to display courage and to embrace life. Your love of simple pleasures, books or movies from Amazon or Etsy, ordering stuff on-line so you'd have a package to look forward to, to stay alive for.

I saw how you lived within your budget. I appreciated the way you brought interesting people into your life with your compassion for those besieged by bad luck. I learned a person could be brilliant and capable and still be stuck in panic, anxiety, and depression and not able to function. I learned to set boundaries with you and to appreciate you as you were.

Throughout all those tumultuous years, you were a teacher I never would or could walk away from—a stern, angry, witty, charming, irritable sage full of surprises both welcome and unwelcome.

This to just to say I love you beyond measure and miss you beyond stars.

Love, Mom

Dear Mom,

That is quite a birthday letter. I like reading about how much you learned from me. And me, not even a college graduate. That was yet another thing you had to accept—a university dropout!

It makes me sad that you had to let go of so much. But it also makes me happy to see how much you really love me. Otherwise, you never would have put up with all that.

And now, here we are, in opposite worlds. You sad and yearning; me peaceful and calm. Maybe when a person dies there's a reset button and they erase all your emotions. Or maybe your brain chemicals fall into a healthy place. I wish we could actually be together, in person, right now. You would be amazed how relaxed I am. No drugs. No meds. No cuts. No burns. No chewed fingernails or wild blue unwashed hair. No bouncing knee and impossibly dry mouth from all the meds. No grinding my teeth. No clutching an extra-large Diet Coke so I can get through the hour. Although I wouldn't mind a Diet Coke right now.

I love you too, Mom, and always have, despite all the terrible things I've said and done. I believe you know that but want to make sure. That way, you can still celebrate your anniversary of being a mother in the style you've become accustomed to.

Love, Your Other-Worldly Daughter, Hilee

Dear Hilee,

Thank you for your beautiful letter.

Here's how your birthday unfolded:

I wake up and you are still dead. Or, if you are not dead—as I secretly hope and suspect—you are inaccessible as far as ordinary communication goes.

After I write to you, I sit in the dining room and stare into space.

The grandchildren are having a sleepover and when they wake up, Annabelle plays school, complete with wearing fake glasses and going over a lesson plan. The first time she put on the glasses, she instantly took them off and told me, "Don't worry. It's still me!" Then put them back on so she could be a proper teacher.

Robert and Ron make us breakfast: fruit-laden oatmeal and *Beyond* breakfast sausages, which means no meat. If you were here, I'd try to trick you into eating one. You might think, *Am I eating Jimmy Dean's?* Or you might think, *Oh my God, my poor mother is deluded.*

When we take the children home, Sarah comes outside and she is as sad as I am. As Judith Viorst might say, it's a "terrible, horrible, no good, very bad day."

Returning home, I sit on the futon, facing the guinea pig habitat. That way, I can stare into space and see adorable little animals chewing hay, grooming, and sleeping. That feels quite comforting.

Then, your Uncle Dan texts. Like a scene from childhood, my little brother wants to show us his new toy. This adds a splash of surrealism to the morning. He drives over, goes into his workshop that Ron has created for him in our ancient car-free garage, and we wait expectantly for "the big reveal."

While we wait, guess what I do? Right—stare into space. Then Dan invites us into the garage to see his fabulous new machine—the Lichtenburg Fractal Wood Burner. It's a magic etching device for wood. Dan sends us back into the house so he can have artistic freedom. Soon he comes in bearing two boards with his artwork on them, delicate Asian-inspired tree limbs trembling across the wood. Beautiful! It's a lovely distraction.

Now for the birthday lunch. For some years, you and I dined at Johnny Cascone's monthly. During COVID, I went there for carry-out and delivered lunch to you. I haven't been there since you died, and it feels strange to walk in. But one thing about this old Italian restaurant—it doesn't change.

Ron and I arrive early, and they have our table properly set up, complete with a wise-mouthed waiter whose best childhood friend was named Shouse. He recites a list of Shouses, in case I know any of them. I feel like stuffing a loaf of bread into his mouth.

Hilee, you would have liked this gathering. Me, Ron, cousin Janet, Dan and Dena, Sarah, Jeff, Robert, and Annabelle. Dan thought Mom and Dad would enjoy being part of this memorial meal, so he had them pay for it out of the fund they left for important family gatherings. When he announces that they are part of the celebration, Sarah and I both cry; it is so sweet and tender.

Then, Dan says, "Get whatever you want." You would have been all over that incredible offer. But can you believe this: no one even orders a dessert? You would have broken that barrier. Lemon cake? Tiramisu? Or possibly, on this momentous occasion, both! Carry-out, of course.

We talk about the crossword puzzle trip that you and Sarah and I took to NYC, our family reunion trip in Arkansas, that amazing Chicago experience with Mom and Dad when they got to stay at the site of their wedding reception, the esteemed Palmer House, for free! We talk about the period when you were doing Tae Bo, working, going out dancing with Sarah.

All of this in Cascone's, our family restaurant.

Your dad loved it too and we went there several times together, even after we were divorced.

Later in the afternoon, I walk with Sarah. We both miss you enormously.

As I drive home from Sarah's house, KCUR plays an old song by Sly and the Family Stone, one I've never heard: *Crossword Puzzles*. I can't believe it.

In the evening, I watch *Queer Eye*. They feature a makeover for a 67-year-old Cajun restauranteur, whose wife had died ten years earlier. It is all about honoring the dead, but not getting stuck in the grief. Moving forward without disrespecting the past. Carrying your loved ones with you but remembering to take care of your own dear self. It is the perfect ending to this difficult, emotional day.

But wait! There's more! I had a cupcake set aside and I light a birthday candle for you. Ron and I think about you and send you many blessings.

Even though it is a vegan, gluten-free cupcake, it is filled with sugar, and I think you would have liked it: chocolate with a gooey caramel filling and a fluffy vanilla "cream" frosting.

So Hilee, I spent your birthday with you. Although in real life, you never would have made it through such a long day and would have probably just come to lunch, taken your leftovers, and headed home. One good thing about your being dead, if indeed you are dead: I get to spend as much time with you as I want!

With love, love, love, Mom

Dear Mom,

I'm glad to hear about my birthday celebration. You are extremely optimistic, assuming I would have shown up for lunch. With that many people, I might have been tempted to "develop a cold," and beg you to deliver my meal!

Another good thing about being dead: you no longer have to disappoint people. Sure, they're sad, but they don't blame you for your death, do they?

I listened to that Crossword Puzzles song. Guess what—all I had to do was think the words and it played in my mind. Now I know why we never heard of it—not so catchy as *We Are Family*.

If you hadn't mentioned my birthday, I wouldn't have even known. No days, no time here. But since you told me it was an auspicious day, I did open the manual to page 4.

These people need to learn to write a sentence. It said, BU. At first, I thought it was an endorsement for Boston University. Then I thought, "Birthday Up." Or "Birthday Unique." I wish it had said, "BS." That I would have understood.

Meanwhile, time to fly. Where is Tinker Bell when you need her?

Love, Hilee

Dear Mom,

Okay, Mom, you will not believe this. The moment I wrote about Tinker Bell, she popped into my head and offered me pixie dust. I was so freaked out I thought of Captain Hook, and she disappeared. Then I had to think of the crocodile to get rid of Hook. Then, well, I closed my eyes and counted my breaths, and all was calm.

Love, Hilee

Dear Hilee,

That is remarkable. You have more superpowers than you know. And I'm not being metaphorical. I think the sky's the limit.

Can you fly down to Earth?

What if BU is a corny way of saying "Be Yourself?"

Love, Mom

Dear Mom,

Would they really do that, use a U when they really meant a Y? Isn't that against the Golden Rule and the Ten Commandments, along with *Robert's Rules of Order* and *Strunk & White?*   Love, Hilee

Dear Hilee,

When you were alive, you didn't possess the free attention to hear about my issues and challenges. But now, you seem more open to knowing me. Perhaps hearing about my sense of loss and devastation will help you understand the depths of my caring for you.

What a morning of sorrow. Your death is intolerable, eroding my heart. I lie in bed unable to move, literally laden with grief.

Inside I am screaming, "I want my daughter back!" Externally, I am silently sobbing. When my tears turn to stones, I pry myself up and zombie into my clothes. I walk downstairs and feed the guinea pigs their breakfast of lettuce and red peppers. I listen to their serious, rhythmic chewing and pet their soft fur. I smile at their excitement over new hay. Each time I put a small handful into their container, they run over, eager to sample, nibble, enjoy. I love their unbridled enthusiasm for the familiar.

Yesterday, a friend told me, "You are so resilient."

I thanked her. But maybe I am just good at walking a tightrope over my grief.

I wonder if I'm going to be happier now that your birthday is over. I so wanted you to be happier. Now, I want that for myself.

Is this just the circle of life or is it the circle of co-dependence?   Love, Mom

Dear Mom,

Co-dependence, that's your thing. Prove that you love me, that was my thing. Maybe manifesting my own clothes and books takes the place of needing so much from people.

Guess what! I used the Stuff on Earth channel to look at my darling dog Muddy. Remember how he used to jump the fence and escape? Now, he's racing around in a giant yard. It's like a pet food commercial. And guess who was there, petting Muddy, throwing a beat-up ball? Matthew. And he didn't have a girlfriend with him. Good thing. I was so glad to see him. I really do believe we were good for each other.

The breathing and meditating has lost its glow. I'm going to concentrate on flying.

Love, Hilee Up High

Dear Hilee,

Today, cousin Zach sent me an email, asking if I thought your death was "unjust."

Then he wrote, "Want to discuss?"

I did. Ever since my mother died, almost 20 years ago now, I have been interested in discussing death. Being with her while she died was a powerful experience and it soothed much of my fear about dying.

This evening, Zach and I talked. I told him that at first I thought your death was unfair, because you were finally looking forward, feeling hopeful about living. Your death was also ironic. For so many years, you threatened suicide and experimented with ways to harm yourself. But the last few years, you seemed more at peace. Is that true? Were you peaceful or was it the drugs? Or does it even matter?

Love, Mom

Dear Mom,

Peace, drugs, and rock and roll—it's all the same.

If you think too much about the drugs, you're going to feel guilty. And why should you feel guilty? You probably haven't tried many drugs, so you don't know how intriguing they are.

Just be happy I am peaceful. That sounds rather Buddhist, don't you think? If I start sounding enlightened, will you arrange for an intervention?

Ommmm,

Hilee Krishna

Hilee Krishna, Hilee Krishna, Krishna Krishna, Hilee, Hilee,

Love, H.K.

Dear Hilee,

At 5:45 this morning, while I was still asleep, someone whispered, "Mom. Mom!"

Was that you?   Love, Mom

Dear Mom,

I cannot reveal my whereabouts in the morning's early hours.

Mysteriously, Hilee

Dear Hilee,

This morning, I am listening to the patter of little feet: the guinea pigs are playing tag in their habitat. When I come downstairs in the morning, they are "standing like statues," staring at me, like monks by the side of the road, patiently holding their begging bowls. Juno and Coco don't have quite as much fortitude as the monks. They will eventually start wheeking and gnawing at the bars of their habitat, eager to eat their delicious daily lettuce.

Grief is like the old gray sweatshirt I keep putting on, even when I have a closet full of other more colorful clothes.

Love, Mom

Dear Mom,

You are good at rising above things. But are you good at sinking in and being patient? Me thinks, not so much.

Nothing wrong with wearing the same clothes over and over again. Remember Georgia O'Keefe's long black dress that she wore every day for a week!

I, on the other hand, am wearing hot pink leggings with rhinestones and a silky, navy-blue pirate-type top, with a gold belt. It may sound tacky, but it looks surprisingly good. I'm leaving my bubble and I'll see how it flies.

If you see a hot pink blur in the sky,
You will know—it is I.

Love, Hilee

Dear Mom,

Would you believe, I found a group of souls who are trying to fly. I was bouncing along like an uncoordinated joey, and I bumped into someone! It was like two helium balloons hitting against each other, just a gentle tap. The being I bumped was dressed like Snow White, but her stomach-curdling laugh was loud and witchy. I felt like Dorothy when she first met the wicked witch. I wanted to get back to Kansas, pronto.

Then the being said, "Hey, got anything to smoke?"

I did. Mom, up here, people do not give you dirty looks when you smoke. Probably they're thinking, "It's your death." Anyhow, Mom, when you die, I highly recommend you try smoking. It's fabulous.

Before I could manifest a cigarette, she said, "Follow me." We bumbled along and found at least 20 others, all leaping about like they were in a field of pogo sticks.

"This is the try-fly zone," she said.

Being around others who were jumping made me leap higher. Someone wearing a flight suit called out, "Don't move your arms so much. Don't try so hard — it's weighing you down. Just relax, leap, and imagine connecting with an air current or cloud."

I wanted to say, "You do know that clouds are just unrealized rain, don't you? Nothing really there to connect with."

But I didn't want to be a smart-ass. So, I stopped whirring around my arms, closed my eyes, took a breath, and jumped. I went higher but I got scared and crashed. But not to worry: I wasn't hurt.

That's as far as I got, because even dead, I don't like to be around people for long swaths of time. Still, pretty exciting, huh.

Love, High-lee

Dear High-lee,

Very exciting. Thrilling even. And to think you don't need to flap your arms!

Sending love, Mom

Dear Hilee,

Beautiful snow here, supposed to drift down all day. I hope I will go outside and make my footprints.

Last time, I stayed inside, because it was impossibly cold.

Dorothy Parker was a *Jeopardy* clue yesterday. The answer was related to the word "dust" in her epitaph. It's your kind of poem, Hilee.

> *Epitaph for a Darling Lady*
> (Verse three)
> "Leave for her a red young rose,
> Go your way, and save your pity;
> She is happy, for she knows
> That her dust is very pretty."

In my younger years, I was very influenced by Dorothy because of "Men seldom make passes/At girls who wear glasses." Even with your dad, I didn't wear my glasses in front of him until the day before our wedding. Is that why they say, "Love is blind?"

My favorite Dorothy Parker is this piece of wisdom:

> "Oh, life is a glorious cycle of song,
> A medley of extemporanea,
> And love is a thing that can never go wrong,
> And I am Marie of Romania."

It's not just romantic love that can never go wrong. Right? It's nice to have something in common with Queen Marie of Romania.

Love, Mom

Dear Mom,

I love thinking about all those cynical and witty writers, drinking Manhattans and martinis and talking, talking, talking around the Algonquin Round Table. Maybe I'll dress like Dorothy Parker some day and see if I attract any bitter intellectuals.

I'm having a little personal argument, once again plucking daisy petals, saying, "Loves me, Loves me not." Only mine is, "I can fly, I'm terrified to fly. I can fly. I'm terrified…"

This is a big deal, a puzzle I need to figure out, particularly since there's nothing that resembles soil, dirt, or "pretty dust" here.

I was so discombobulated by the possibility of flying that I opened the manual. Again.

Page 5. LET GO OF WHAT YOU KNOW.

I have no idea what this manual is supposed to be about.

Love, H

Dear Hilee,

I hope that doesn't mean letting go of me and Sarah. It does seem like you've been shedding a lot of your toxic emotional patterns, which is excellent news.

I'm pretty sure I'd be scared, too, if I could almost fly. When you see the group again, maybe you will get tips on landing.

It's either love or the territorial imperative, the way Coco purrs and sashays around, and Juno squeaks at her. Or maybe it's just entertainment, interjecting some jazz into their relationship.

Here in Kansas City, we are going to make scones with Robert and Annabelle. We are reviewing our income taxes and hoping we will return our overdue library books. And we are wondering if you are already flying overhead. Notice I am using the royal "we." Seeing if writing in that imperialistic way would lift my spirits. The answer is no.

I can imagine someone reading this and saying, "Deborah, you need a hobby." Is writing to you my hobby? Or my temporary lifeline?

Love, Mom

Dear Mom,

I am spending the day under three pink blankets with a big cuddly trouble-free dog.

Normally, I like to tune into *Stuff on Earth*, but today I'm setting down the remote. Did I tell you? You cannot lose the remote! It instantly appears when you need it. I'm going to reread Stephen King's *Carrie*. God, I loved that movie. I know, I know, the blood scene was way too much for you, not to mention the super scary and utterly thrilling ending.

Anyway, even up here I need time to lie abed. So don't bother looking up in the sky for me today. I am definitely grounded.

Love, Hilee

Dear Hilee,

Yesterday, I told my therapist: "I'm on a mission from God," (to quote the Blues Brothers) regarding writing letters to you. Even though writing to you makes me sad, I also feel connected. Sometimes I wonder, should I move on, make myself write about something else, start a story, a novel, an essay? But I am ill-inclined. This appears to be my current calling and sorrow is my calling card.

I like that last sentence; a bit melodramatic but with a nice flair, don't you think?

Love, Mom

Dear Mom,

Maybe that can be the title of your next book: *Sorrow Is My Calling Card*. Makes me think of the *Thin Man* characters, Nick and Nora and Asta. Remember back when Asta was a frequent crossword puzzle clue?

Love, Hilee

Dear Hilee,

I always got that clue right, unlike today, when I don't know many of the cultural references.

Yesterday I felt stressed because I had too many appointments, most of them to see people I really wanted to see. But I am used to the isolation of the pandemic and being social still feels alien. Especially more than once or twice a week!

I'll bet you felt that way a lot.

Love, Mom

Dear Mom,

I felt that way most of the time. Even the idea of seeing you or Sarah or cousin Janet, people I didn't have to perform or be cheerful for, could totally panic me. But in a way, I did have to perform. I had to be reasonably clean and articulate. I had to be part of a conversation. Some days, that was like appearing on a London stage as Lady Macbeth, so overwhelming, so draining, the show just couldn't go on. Does that make sense?

I don't feel that way anymore. Of course, nobody knows me or expects anything from me here.

Love, Hilee

Dear Hilee,

You gave yourself purple hair but maybe you really deserved a Medal of Valor, for bravery in the face of the everyday battle. It makes me so sad thinking of all your struggles.

Love, Mom

Dear Mom,

Right now, everything makes you sad. Isn't there some famous Italian guy who says, "Forget about it?"

Forget about it. It's over. I could rise up from these blankets any time I want and probably even fly.

Can you believe, I only know the names of a couple of beings here? I'm usually friendlier than that, but maybe I was friendly because I wanted people to like me. Or I wanted the "appearance of being normal." Now, I don't really care. Is that maturity or ennui? (Don't you love that word, "ennui?")

If you thought you could fly, would you start trying today?

Love, Hilee, Low on the Ground

Dear Hilee,

I would probably make a long list of to-dos, put "learn to fly" on it and then think about flying for a day or two, without taking any action.

Sending love, Mom

Dear Hilee,

Suddenly, I feel like we're out of touch. Is that true? I sit down to write, and I don't know what to say.

The idea of not writing to you is big and lonely. Having a dead pen pal is a surprisingly comforting experience. If we're not writing, an abyss will crack open my heart.

Everyone seems to know this about grieving: you move forward and then you fall backwards. You're functioning and then you're mired in sorrow. I have vowed to be in the flow, regarding our post-life relationship. I have glibly said, "I'll know when it's time to stop writing."

Is it time? The mere thought makes me shiver. What will I do when I wake up in the morning? How will I keep you with me? But maybe you are supposed to move on. Maybe I am supposed to move on.

What I'm trying to say is, "Don't leave me yet. I'm not ready."

Love, Mom

Dear Mom,

I don't want to leave you. This writing business is pretty cool. But I know what you mean, and I don't know what to do about it. Nothing is different really; I haven't received any secret notes from on-high or anything. Yet I feel our connection is fading.

Meanwhile, I've lost all my steam. Maybe that's what you feel. But let's not worry yet. Maybe we just need a break. If you still want to write, go ahead. I am lying here with my head under the blankets, but I can probably still read your letters.

Love, Hilee

Dear Hilee,

Hmmm, the idea that you might or might not read my letters is quite demoralizing. But I will keep writing as I need to. I'm stopping for today to lie down and feel sad.

Sending love, Mom

Dear Hilee,

Maybe a cosmic power is pulling away our mutual mojo. My energy is flat. As I got out of bed this morning, I said to Ron, "It's going to be a happy day." A quote from Annabelle's adaptive dance class. But I didn't really mean it. Besides your various comfort foods, the people you love, and Muddy, what do you miss about your "so-called life" on Earth?   Love, Mom

Dear Mom,

I miss shouting. Conflict. Misery. Worry. Anger— beautiful righteous roaring fury. Standing on the edge of a dark pit and almost falling in. That's what I miss. Sometimes. Other times, I am content to be in this calm setting, having my alleged "rest and rejuvenation."

Now that I'm dead, you probably don't have much shouting and anger in your life. Don't you miss it? A little, at least?

Love, Hilee

Dear Hilee,

I miss you, but I don't miss your anger. Remember the time you were furious with me, and you begged me to yell at you? And I shouted, "Fuck you, Hilee!" You were so happy. I have to admit, it felt pretty good to scream that out. Although I felt guilty afterward. Only a little, though.

Why were you angry at me so often?

Love, Mom

Dear Mom,

Sometimes I resented the super rational way you talked to me. I thought you didn't care about me. Dad was so different—he'd shout insulting things and I'd yell back and get mad and cry and then he'd feel bad and apologize. It was quick as dynamite and very cleansing.

But I couldn't talk to you like that—you would have disintegrated. I always thought it was important to stay on Dad's good side. Otherwise, he might get pissed off and leave. Or stop supporting me. You might get pissed off, but you'd never leave. At least I didn't think you would.

Love, Hilee

Dear Hilee,

I had some moments when I understood why parents disown their children. But I would never leave you.

Ultimately, you didn't need to worry, since you ended up leaving me. And the rest of us. Sometimes missing you is a piece of carry-on luggage; other times I'm lugging a huge steamer trunk.

Maybe I'm grateful I didn't know about the drugs. Maybe I'm not. That was an important part of your life and I would have liked to know when and why you started using, what drugs you preferred, how you got the drugs, who you were using with, and why there were needles all over your house. So many unanswered questions.

But, harkening back to your sage advice from weeks ago, "Ha ha ha, nothing matters."

Although I do think love matters.

Love, Mom

Dear Mom,

Naturally you think that love matters. But in my humble opinion, love isn't nearly enough to sustain a person through life's perils. You need grit and anger and hustle and desire.

See why I couldn't tell you about the drugs? You are way too curious. When a person is using, they don't want to answer such questions. At least I didn't. I just wanted to escape.

Sorry if I let you down in that way. But I did what I needed to do.

Love, Hilee

Dear Hilee,

I'm not mad you didn't tell me about the drugs. I'm just sad that I knew so little about you and your life.

Love, Mom, the curious

Dear Hilee,

At some point, I would like to talk about your wedding. That was a sore spot in our lives, wasn't it? Me, trying to please you and wanting to have the wedding here, so we could celebrate with friends and family. You getting all insulted for some reason, and arranging for the wedding in Florida. That was such a blow. But I knew if I tried to persuade you to stay in town, you would find fault with everything I did. Right?

As it was, Carlton's mom did an excellent job of arranging things. The venue was so festive, and it was a lovely ceremony. You looked fabulous with your sparkling red shoes and blue gingham dress. We took pictures of it all, and you never wanted to look at them, ever. Why was that?

Sending love, Mom

Dear Mom,

I do want to talk about the wedding, but not now. Now, I am going to open up Page 6 of the manual. Drum roll!

LET GO OF WHAT YOU THINK YOU KNOW.

Didn't we just do that one?

Still, pretty appropriate, wouldn't you say?

Love, Hilee

Dear Hilee,

The older I get, the less adamant I am about what I think I know. For example, I think a lot about growing

122

older, wondering if I need more of a plan, wondering what that plan would be.

Right now, I am healthy and my version of strong. But things could change, and I worry I don't have a big enough support system. Your earthly presence offered me comfort, even though I knew you wouldn't necessarily help me if I became infirm.

We had a cardinal at our safflower feeder last night. Weeks ago, a friend had told me, "I think Hilee is flying around as a cardinal."

You don't seem like the redbird type, but I still greeted the bird, saying, "Hi, Hilee." It was pleasant to say hello to you.

Love, Mom

Dear Mom,

Maybe my presence in the spirit world will offer more comfort than I ever could on Earth.

If I learn to fly, I doubt I'd flitter about as a puny cardinal. I'd swoop in as a raven or an eagle or one of those air-current riding hawks.

"Hope is a thing with feathers." Remember that Emily Dickinson line? Remember that essay you wrote, comparing me to Emily? Did I ever tell you—I really liked that piece?

Maybe after I get rid of all my earthly baggage, I'll be able to soar.   Love, Hilee

Dear Mom,

I bounced yesterday. I was wandering around, wishing I could find the flying people and there they were. Maybe because I was thinking about them.

Anyway, one of the souls, an old, old woman dressed in flowing white, helped me bounce. An angel? A ghost? A combo of the two?

Her voice sounded like tinkling bells. I wonder what my voice sounds like.

She put her hands on my waist and told me to jump up. I did and she boosted me, so I went pretty high, then bounced when I landed. I had to wave my arms to keep my balance.

She kept helping me until I could do it myself. So, bouncing is the first step to flying.

Love, Hilee the Bouncer

Dear Hilee,

Hooray for taking those first leaps into the air!

It's amazing how you created a relationship without ever leaving your room, inspiring a grown man to drive non-stop from Orlando to Overland Park to meet you. Carlton was so smitten with you! Emily D might have enjoyed such a dalliance, had it been available to her. That essay about you and Emily is a pure ode of admiration to your creativity and charisma.

Love, Mom

Dear Mom,

I am creative and persistent, aren't I? Some might say, "pestery" but I prefer "determined."

I am still adjusting to having everything I want and need. When I was alive, I felt I didn't deserve anything, and I had to fight for what I needed. Sounds silly, I know, coming from a person who had her rent royally subsidized, and handyman help when needed. Plus, friends and relatives willing to assist. But I lived with the feeling of "nobody loves me." I depended on the kindness of family members. Which is more reliable, but more emotionally fraught, than the "kindness of strangers," right? Maybe the feeling of being unloved grew from all those years Dad used to say, "Nobody will ever love you as much as I do." I think he said that to you too, didn't he?

Now, being loved doesn't seem necessary for survival. It's eerie, Mom, to be feeling this way. But it's also semi-wonderful.

Love, Hilee

Dear Hilee,

When I was a kid, I thought I had to be loved in order to survive. Quite a precarious and stressful feeling.

Yes, Larry used to tell me no one would ever love me as much as he did. But after a while, I began to think, maybe that was a good thing. His love was so laden with demands, so heavy, so territorial. It was a relief not to be loved so much.

Do you agree?

Love, Mom

April, Inviting Grief to Pass Over

Hilee and I are now writing each other in such a deep way. She is no longer worried about disappointing me. I am no longer scared of angering her. We are asking each other questions and offering blunt and heart-felt answers. Hilee writes: "Our relationship is both happily and unhappily ever after, which is far more sustainable than putting such a stress on pure happiness. And if I'm not in the "ever after" stage, who is!"

Dear Mom,

Let's talk about my wedding.

I was so upset and confused during that time. Carlton loved me. I loved him. He wanted to marry me. He needed to be married. I wanted to prove that someone loved me, that I wouldn't be an old maid, that someone cared enough to propose and make me his wife.

Maybe you're thinking, *Weren't you a feminist, Hilee?*

I was a feminist who wanted to get married. I didn't say I wanted to BE married, just GET married. I wanted the presents and the attention and a pretty dress, hair and make-up, and all the glamour. Mom, you have to admit, you are not particularly a glamour goddess.

Something you said pissed me off—even after you offered a reception with BBQ and pretty much everything we asked for. Maybe I was mad at Carlton. Maybe I was mad at myself. But it was more cathartic to get mad at you. And taking the reception away from you was a powerful thing to do. So, I did it. I'm not proud of that. I know it hurt you deeply.

When I called Carlton's mom, she instantly phoned her friends, found a venue, engaged a preacher, I mean she was on it! She was so excited about Carlton getting married! She wanted it!

You didn't want it. I mean, you weren't against it, but you wondered why did we need to get married?

Anyhow, looking back, I can see you were very understanding, that your feelings were shattered when I yanked away the wedding from you, that you rallied and invited other family to help celebrate, that you were super nice to Carlton's mom, and that you supported me in every way. So that's my side.

Love, Hilee

Dear Hilee,

I appreciate your perspective on the wedding. It's

nice to talk to each other without getting upset, isn't it? You and I have a lot in common, even though our differences are stark. But the more I know you, the more I understand. I saw how much you yearned for validation. You had a vision and you manifested it.

Oh well, even if I didn't get to host your wedding celebration, I got to help you with your divorce. Not every girl gets to go to divorce court with her mom. Remember the woman ahead of us, how horrible her husband was? You and I had a moment of gratitude, whispering that at least you had a place to live, a family, enough money. But the courtroom experience was so draining for you. You didn't even want to go out to eat afterward.

Love, Mom.

Dear Hilee,

One of my friends believes you were in my life for a purpose, maybe to help me become stronger. Part of your own life purpose was to help underdogs and people who were worse off than you were. You were open and generous to those who were struggling, and impatient and dismissive to those who were not. Larry was like that too—he had a huge generous streak but wasn't always nice to the people he "loved." Can you tell I haven't quite forgiven him, that I am still clutching a little grudge?

Love, Mom

Dear Mom,

For a long time, I blamed you for making Dad so sad by divorcing him. You know how Dad was—he probably told me how wonderful he'd been and how you didn't love him anymore. He might have said you didn't love me anymore. But I'm pretty sure I wouldn't have believed that.

Anyhow, those years are a blur. I hated myself. I hated you for letting me live with Dad. For me, it was another sign that you didn't love me enough. I probably even hated Dad for leaning on me so much.

I know, I know. You didn't want me to live with Dad. But I told you I wanted to because Dad wanted me to. I hoped you would rescue me, but you didn't. Probably you couldn't. Dad was pretty crazy back then.

Talking about those times used to really upset me, but now it seems like another lifetime. Well, I guess that's literally true.

Let's talk about something more cheerful.

I am hanging around with the Fly-by-Nights, the name I've given to a bunch of motley souls who want to soar. Already, I can hear you cautioning, "Be careful, Hilee! Don't fly too close to the sun!" Or something like that.

For some reason, I feel more comfortable trying to fly with these beings. Though normally, I don't like to fail around other people. Of course, I generally don't like to fail at all. We help each other bounce. Remember the old, old ghostly woman I told you about? Every time I see her, she gives me a boost. Today I went so high, I nearly bumped my head on a star. Ha ha, just kidding. Even here, the stars are pretty far away. Yesterday she gave me my usual boost, and I wasn't scared. I then gave someone else a boost, and that felt amazing as well.

Something's happening here, Mom, but what it is ain't exactly clear.

Love and a Hilee-five, Hilee

Dear Mom,

I recently read, "A bed with books on it is not unmade." I like hardback books I have read multiple times. I probably take after Dad in that way. You like paperback books, so you don't have to take care of them. But Mom, you really don't have to take care of hardbacks. You can just enjoy them, and they don't mind their spines cracking and their pages doing yoga in the corners. And they love being underlined. It's like having a divine back-scratch.

I do believe I'm going through this enormous letting go period. Shedding mood swings, anxiety, OCD, paranoia, solipsism (great word, huh), doubt. I have a lot to get rid of and I'm just beginning. I lay down my imaginary sense of being unloved. I lay down my prickly feelings of anxiety. I throw down my fucking fogging depression.

Love, and considering laying down my sword and shield,

Hilee

Dear Hilee,

What would it take for you and me to be totally at ease with each other, to fully forgive each other?

I'm not sure of my answer. Over the last couple of years, I have more fully accepted and appreciated you as you are. I did wish you would get your teeth fixed, but that was more about wanting you to be healthy and comfortable. How about you?

Love, Mom

Dear Mom,

While I was alive, I never thought about forgiving you or getting closer to you. You were just there, my mother. I could irritate you, be mean to you. I could apologize, and you would forgive me. You were my comfortable armchair that I didn't mind eating chips in or spilling Diet Coke on.

But I have more perspective since my "tragic and early demise." I can see all the anger that burned inside me, the self-loathing that poisoned me, the dark sense of worthlessness that no amount of appreciation or praise could erase. No wonder I wanted to lose myself in drugs.

I thought you could never understand me, because of all I had gone through, because of how different we were. But I didn't give you credit for being an empathetic person. I'm starting to give you more credit now.

Love, Hilee

Dear Hilee,

Fifty-three years ago today, I walked down the aisle of our family den in Memphis, toward the Rabbi and Larry Robert Shouse. Toward marriage. I carried a small bouquet of daisies and wore an ivory-colored floor-length dress that cost $100.00, the most money anyone in our family had ever spent on clothing. My Uncle Lou, a professional photographer, took our wedding photos. It was a spring-break gathering, put together in a week because Larry had just received his draft notice. Larry and I were in deep love, and we had to be together. I wanted to go to Fort Rucker, Alabama, with him, but my parents would have been aghast and ashamed if we had lived together without the sanctity of marriage.

The city was under curfew, because a year earlier Martin Luther King had been assassinated in Memphis and the police were expecting trouble. So, we had to end our celebration by 7:30.

This is part of your origin story, Hilee—two people in deep crazy love.

Love, Mom

Dear Mom,

Here's what I'm thinking about you and me: our relationship is both happily and unhappily ever after, which is far more sustainable than putting such a stress on pure happiness. And if I'm not in the "ever after" stage, who is!

It's strange thinking of you and Dad being young and in big crazy love.

Happy Former Anniversary.

Love, Hilee

Dear Hilee,

Our first date, Larry and I walked around half the night talking. Larry recited poetry and carried me on his shoulders. It was the longest walk we ever took! Later he told me he was trying to get me to like him. It worked!

Love, Mom

Dear Mom,

By the way, I just read page 7 of the Manual. TASTE RISK. What in the world is that supposed to mean? Maybe it's the appetizer for Take Risks?

Love, Hilee

Dear Hilee,

You are a lot better at tasting risk than I am. You are learning to soar, while I struggle to pull back my shoulders, raise my head, and stand up straight. Before the COVID, I was doing posture exercises. When the plague came, I thought I might die. I assumed, "Dead people don't need good posture."

Now that I'm probably going to live, straightening up could be a grand idea.

While you are bouncing, Sarah is running. Tomorrow she is competing in her first half-marathon. We are going to stand on Ward Parkway and applaud as she dashes by!

Someday, we'll look up, see you fly by, and cheer!

Love, Mom

Dear Mom,

You do know you might not be able to actually "see" me, don't you? Even if I were wearing my fancy outfits, I'm not sure you could even notice the clothes.

135

These things are a mystery to me. One I don't particularly want to solve.

I am rather obsessed with flying and with this ancient lady who boosts me off the ground. So, I can barely focus on me or you or what happened all those years ago.

Perhaps you feel my distance. It's not personal. It's something you would approve of: Setting a goal and trying to reach it. Pretty amazing, huh?

Anyhow, keep writing but do not despair if you don't hear from me right away. I'm trying to be uplifted!

Love, Hilee

Dear Hilee,

How marvelous you have a goal. How exciting you're willing to try, try, again. You didn't get to experience that often during your life. I remember the first time you had to study in school—seventh grade. You had sailed through the other years. Then suddenly, you had to work to comprehend the material. You found this turn of events totally unfair.

Maybe Larry spoiled you by bragging about how smart you were. But it's a burden to have so much intelligence thrust upon you.

Love, Mom

Dear Mom,

I was crushed that I had to study. I took that as a sign of weakness and worried I wasn't as smart as Dad wanted me to be. He seemed so set on my brilliance. I couldn't see my brilliance, but Dad loved it.

Now, there's nobody to please but myself. As it turns out, once you take away the material world and all its splendors, I'm pretty easy to please. Unlike on Earth, where I always felt something was missing.

Is this the way regular people feel? Maybe I would never have taken drugs if I hadn't felt so anxious, worried, and empty. But maybe I would have, for the daring and fun of it. We'll never know, will we?

Mom, I don't regret taking the drugs. Except how sad it made you and Sarah. But I never think, *Oh, I wish I'd never tasted those evil substances.* They definitely have their own charms, as millions of addicts can tell you.

Was I an addict? I don't think so. Not yet at least. But I could have become one. And I probably would have enjoyed that. At least half the time. Anyway, those distresses and stresses are gone. Time to take to the skies!

Love, Hilee

Dear Hilee,

Since you rarely attended holiday celebrations, I don't feel sorrowful that you're not attending now.

Take Passover, coming up this Friday. Last year, you and I actually had a good talk about the holiday. I encouraged you to stop pretending you would attend, then backing out at the last minute.

You finally told me, "I don't want to come." That definitive answer was quite helpful. I could then tamp down my fantasy about having my two daughters at Seder.

So this year, while I may not miss you so much on Friday evening, I will miss our conversations about whether you're coming!

Love, Mom

Dear Mom,

I only like the part of ceremony where the leader reads the list of things God did for the Jews and we all get to yell "Dayenu!" a million times. What a word — Dayenu: "It would have been enough." Though, until now, I rarely thought anything was ever Dayenu.

When I was little, I also liked the part of the Seder when Pauly hid a couple scrawny pieces of Matzo in the living room, symbolizing who knows what, and at the end of the meal, Sarah and I got money for finding them. But once you're past a certain age, that fun is over. Why is that?

Love, Hilee

Dear Hilee,

Yes, why do people assume that older people don't want special treats? Who doesn't want a lollipop when you visit the bank? A toy after a dental visit? A free cookie when you go to the grocery store?

I'll bet if you interviewed one hundred adults, most would welcome a little treat for doing these tasks. Probably some John Adams type sneaked an "Adults don't want treats" mandate into an obscure part of the Constitution and it stuck.

Love, Mom

Dear Hilee,

I've been thinking about all the mistakes a mother can make. Innocent unfiltered reactions can haunt a child for eons. I'm sure I blurted out remarks like that to you. I know I've apologized, but have you forgiven me?

I am thinking about this because of a reaction from my mother when I was twelve has involuntarily shaped my self-image and my thinking. Yesterday in counseling I worked on this. Here's the scene. Mom and I are going school clothes shopping, which was a big deal because I usually wore my cousins' and friends' hand-me-downs. So, buying something new was fantastic!

I tried on a skirt I really liked, and I was gazing at myself in the mirror, thinking, *This looks good.*

Then Mom came into the dressing room and stared at me, her face stern. She said, "That's too tight. You can't wear that!"

In my pre-teen mind, she was saying, "You look fat." Being overweight was a sin in her mind. I felt like burrowing into the ground.

Looking back, I think she was dismayed that I was "developing" and that scared her. During therapy, as Eve guided me through a meditative introspection, that memory flashed into my mind. Suddenly Mom was next to me, saying, "I didn't mean to hurt you."

At that moment, I realized Mom was sad, she'd been sad a lot of her life, losing her mother early and then her first husband. I felt this huge empathy for her. A river of forgiveness flowed between us. I understood each of us had been doing our best. It was a healing experience.

Then I wondered if I said anything hurtful to you when you were a pre-teen.

Love, Mom

Dear Mom,

It's nice of you to ask. But if you'd said anything mean to me, I surely would have complained about it years ago. I am not shy about proclaiming perceived injustices.

Sometimes, I feel lonely here. Not despairing, sobbing loneliness; more like a sense of loss. Maybe they program us so we're not mopey and weepy. I wish I'd known that formula when I was alive.

I do miss you all, but I don't mourn over it.

News from above: My friend Lothar has moved in next door. Although really there's no actual door. His bubble is nearby, and he likes to come over and chat. He thinks I'm interesting. I think he's super interesting. So, we are talking a lot. Not just about our previous lives, not just swapping stories like we would if we were on a date. We are talking about how we became who we are.

Yes, I know, isn't that unusual? I never much cared for analysis of feelings and childhood blah blah blah. But with Lothar, it's like putting together a puzzle instead of confessing sins. He reminds me of Quinn, my skinny, hyped up, explosive, magnetic boyfriend Quinn. Only Lothar is calm. I am now calm.

He likes to smoke cigarettes. Oh God, so do I. He always has cigarettes. So, we smoke and talk. It's not about regrets; it's about deductions.

For both of us, our dads are our biggest influencers, perhaps not in a good way. Our moms are anchors. Sorry, Mom, I know you'd rather be an influencer. But

Dad was more persuasive; he threatened he'd stop loving me if I didn't do what he wanted. Lothar's dad was the same, only physically abusive as well.

So, I'm going deep emotionally while trying to float above it all. Nice dichotomy, right?

Love, Hilee

Dear Hilee,

You're right; I yearned to be your influencer. I knew you'd be happier and saner if you'd listen to me. But it's all cosmic, isn't it? I'm interested in hearing anything you learn about yourself.

That's part of what Uncle Dan and I have been doing when we have our weekly talks. We tiptoe into our pasts and think about why and who and what happened. Did you and Sarah ever do this?

Last night, Coco, the queen guinea pig, put her little feet on my hand, and tried to walk up my arm. She looked into my eyes, like she was seeking an important answer. Actually, I think she was just wanting to be next to her sister Juno, who was in a cuddle cave in my lap. But her feet and her trusting gaze melted me. Thank heavens for those moments of melting, or we'd all be too crusty and defensive.

Love, Mom

Dear Hilee,

I woke up with these words in my head: *Why hasn't she written me?* Then I thought, *Why haven't I written her?*

If you get to be reborn, what kind of life would you like to have?

Sending love, Mom

Dear Mom,

I am not in the mood to relocate to the Midwest. But if I have to return, I'd like to be happier and healthier. No giant depressions or anxieties. No eating disorders. But being a typical normal person is not appealing. Maybe I'd have a job as a clothing designer or an artist. But not a super-successful artist. I don't want to be famous, but I want enough money to buy pretty things. On sale, getting a bargain, of course. I'd like to have a really good boyfriend, like Matthew, but better. And Mom, I wouldn't mind taking street drugs or alcohol, at least for a little while. Then I'd triumphantly overcome my addiction.

When you open the door during the Seder service to let in Elijah, I might come floating in. Of course, you won't see me. But watch the levels of your wine glasses. I might be thirsty.

Love, Hilee

Dear Hilee,

I know you remember that important philosophic tome from your childhood, but it bears repeating: "Never tease a weasel." Never tease a Jewish mother about showing up on an esteemed holiday!

I can't imagine you being anything other than an eclectic personality. Perhaps you could be a mistress of the dark arts? But I am surprised that you're interested in being addicted "for a while." Doesn't that guarantee struggle and heartbreak?

Love, Mom

Dear Mom,

You've given me a great idea. I'll be a professional dominatrix. Maybe even in a big city like NYC or DC. That would actually be fun. Although that profession makes it tough to have a really good boyfriend. By the way, no more getting married!

This whole being dead experience is strange. I've lost part of myself and then found another part. My earthly survival tactics—my anger, my stellar manipulation skills, my burning desire to make people prove they loved me, my yearning for gifts and baubles—all are dust. The fact that I can write about this like it's Sunday morning brunch, seems remarkable to me.

Even if I come back to Kansas as a functioning person, I'd never want to have kids. Ever. Too much work.

Too much responsibility. Taking consistent care of someone—that was never my thing. And it's not your fault, Mom. You actually did a decent job.

I am pretty sure I'm in the equivalent of the psycho/addicts neighborhood. But I fit in here. And when we all learn to fly, there'll be a bunch of spooky souls wearing outlandish clothes blocking the sun.

Today I am wearing a magenta sequined top with capped sleeves, tight back leggings with no holes or stains, and shiny patent leather high-heeled boots. So deliciously inappropriate for almost any occasion, unless I was a country music star. I am going to bounce over to the practice field. I mean, why walk in these heels?

Love, Hilee

Dear Mom,

I raised my arms and jumped. Then I inclined my upper body and channeled Peter Pan, singing "I'm Flying," and guess what! I hovered. I mean I was above the ground about three feet, and I moved my arms in breast-stroke fashion to go forward. After a few seconds, my feet went back to the ground, and I had to walk after all.

Ten seconds in air—my personal other-worldly record. I am pretty excited!

Love, Hilee

Dear Hilee,

Congratulations on being airborne! I wish I could have seen that.

Last night we had three extra wine glasses on the Passover table: one with wine for Elijah, harbinger of the Messiah; one with water for Miriam, who led the women across the Red Sea; and one with Diet Coke for you. After we opened the door for Elijah, my friend Robin's daughter Lauren turned to me and said, "I think some of Hilee's Coke is gone. I didn't know Hilee well, but I miss her."

That teared me right up. "Thank you, Lauren," I said. "We miss her too."

Hilee, did you happen to visit last night?

Love, Mom

Dear Mom,

I do appreciate the Diet Coke concept, no ice, just the way I like it. But the size of the glass was so small. If you'd gone to Sonic and purchased the extra-large Route 66 Special maybe, just maybe, I might have dropped by. But the fact that I even considered it—*Dayenu*, right?

I always feel happy and a little guilty that you miss me, that you're sad I'm not there. Here's what I have to say: "For me, dying is better than living in LA."

Remember when I returned from LA, because I was literally going crazy? I was so doped up on medication from that psychiatrist who diagnosed me with schizophrenia. Did I look like a zombie? I felt like one—a zombie with no energy to terrorize and devour people.

Love, Hilee

Dear Hilee,

I was so shocked and angry when you shuffled off the plane that day. Your eyes were vacant, your arms limp, your gait robotic. It was horrible. You did look like a zombie. I wanted to shake you and scream, "Where is my daughter?" They'd put you on a strong old-fashioned tranquilizer, Haldol, or something docs used years ago to quiet patients in the mental hospitals.

I instantly found a psychiatrist who weaned you off the dreadful drug, refuted that diagnosis, and gradually helped you to return to yourself.

Maybe now, you understand how much I love you. I'm sure I've been the source of many hurts. I want to know about these, and I also don't want to know, preferring to cling to the illusion that I was a good mother.

Love, The Ex-Zombie's Mom

Dear Mom,

Yes, you hurt me but I've shed all that. Without particularly trying. Pretty handy, huh?

So don't worry. You were a good mom. If some old memory bothers me, I'll let you know.

Perhaps you are wondering: *Is this really Hilee?*

Yes, it is!

You may also be wondering, *Hilee, why couldn't you have been like this when you were alive?*

Answer: I have no clue.

> Love, The Ideal Daughter, except for the
> small issue of being dead.

Dear Hilee,

Yes, there is that detail of your being dead. At first, I thought that would be the end of our relationship. But now I think it's enhancing our connection. I'm not really sure how that's possible. But when I mention our letters to friends, they all seem copacetic with the idea.

I would ask your secret for letting go of grudges and past hurts, which you clung to like moss on a rock when you were here. But I think you'd just say, "Got to die to do it."

I'm not ready for that yet.

> Love, Mom

Dear Mom,

I like "moss on a rock." I did have a rather tenacious spirit, didn't I? I think you admired that.

Here, there's no pressure to be interesting. I never have to justify my existence by bragging about a good job or an excellent education. Remember when I asked you how I could introduce myself to people and you said, "Writer at large." Or, "I'm currently in transition." You told me a story about how impressed you were at a long-ago party, when a woman said, "I don't have a job and I don't want one."

It was nice of you to say that. You also told me that one of the fanciest boys in my high school, rich and Ivy League educated, ended up as a janitor. I'm not sure that made me feel better. I couldn't even hold a job as a night clerk at a sleazy motel. But still, you were trying to boost my tender spirits.

I opened the manual again. To page 8. SPILL THE BEANS. What beans—pinto, kidney, lima? I've been spilling beans by writing to you.

Mom, you used to believe, "If only Hilee could get the right kind of support and counseling, she'd get a job and leave her house and…." But really Mom, if I'd had a real job, not working for Dad or someone he knew, I'd have only kept at it for a couple of months. And I'd have thrown away all my salary on candy or coke or booze or drugs or clothes. It's good you finally accepted me as I was.

> Is that what it means
> To spill the beans?

Ha ha! A poem, a doggerel verse. Now that matters!

Love, Hilee

Dear Hilee,

A doggerel poem is a true gift.

I love the image of "spill the beans."

It's difficult to discuss death with people. I've worried about it many times myself, when talking to someone who's experienced such a deep loss. How to be empathetic without being intrusive, sensitive without being banal.

I try not to surprise people who don't know me by talking about you or your death. When I get asked about you, I like to be straightforward and use strong clear language. "Dead" instead of "passed on." Each time, the word *dead* kicks me in the stomach, but I welcome that shocking reality check. I spill my beans:

My daughter is dead.

My older daughter is dead.

My daughter Hilee died of a drug overdose.

How many times do I need to say those words to truly, utterly believe them?

One of my friends said, "After a long time goes by, you'll be able to think of Hilee and smile instead of feeling so sad"

I told her, "I can already do that because of our letters! Hilee and I have fun writing to each other."

Why weren't we able to do this in everyday life?

I asked my brother Dan if he ever feels guilt. "Not often," he said. "It's not good for me." I admire how rational and matter-of-fact he is. I am that way as well. Except for my emotional, needy, inner child, and my equally emotional, needy, inner Jewish Mother who believes I must make everyone I love happier.

Love, Mom

Dear Mom,

Now that you describe those two inner parts of you, I understand why it was so easy for me to instantly drive you to grief and despair. Not that I was trying for that. Although you never know.

But I also see how hard you tried to help me. I could say, "If I'd listened to you, I might still be alive." But I won't, even though that might be true. I never wanted to be a copy of you—no offense—I love my inner darkness, and I need to express it.

Remember how Dad was so proud of me as a baby because I'd lick hot sauce off his finger and smile. (I don't actually remember that, but it is a family legend.)

I never wanted to be sugary or sweet. And I think I succeeded, don't you?

Sometimes, I do reflect on my life, but the angst is squeezed out of it. I see myself in my adorable Wizard-of-Oz, Dorothy blue-and-white-checked wedding dress and my ruby slippers and I don't think: *I am a love-starved, insecure, mentally unstable person making a terrible mistake.* I just admire the dress and wonder what would have happened if I had clicked my heels and intoned, "There's no place like home."

Did I tell you there are no bugs here? No mosquitos and flies, no cockroaches. Makes sense. There's no dirt. Of course, I didn't deal with insects on Earth because I rarely went outside.

Love, Hilee

Dear Hilee,

One time Ron and I went to a workshop on the East coast. We sat in a large circle and each person had a minute to introduce themselves. For my intro, I amused myself and sang the song from *The Wizard of Oz:* "I come from a star, and Kansas they say is the name of the star."

People looked at me, not knowing how to react. Kansas seemed like an exotic place to those folks from New Hampshire, Massachusetts, New York.

Now, I'm living in Missouri, where the songs aren't as cute.

I had a moment of unbearable happiness just now, while writing to you. I feel so lucky we're still connected!

Love, Mom

Dear Hilee,

Today we watched a cardinal eat a couple bites of crushed potato chip. Then he flew away to a nearby tree and sang about it. Soon he returned to peck up a few more chips and flew to another, higher branch to serenade us. I've never seen any creature have such joy from a snack food.

A great reminder to savor the small things.

Love, Mom

Dear Hilee,

This morning, I woke up feeling sad. The loss of you is always with me and today I feel it acutely. Maybe because I learned my old friend Judith is quite ill. A year ago, her 50-year-old daughter dropped dead right in front of her. The cause: an overdose of opioids and fentanyl. Just thinking about that makes me want to curl into a ball and stay there forever.

I am so grateful I didn't have to see you die, didn't have to feel the horror and helplessness of not being able to save you. It was terrifying enough seeing you on your lawn covered by a tarp, the police tramping around, the emergency vehicles lining the street, lights flashing.

The sadness rains through me. People say grief is fluid and surprising and you never know when it might envelop you. Today, I am enveloped. Then, as if by magic, I receive an email from a friend who is living with dementia and ALS. She cannot talk, but she can write. She sends a poem about gratitude, and I am reminded how much I have, even in the midst of this terrible, horrible, no good, very bad loss.

Love, Mom

Dear Mom,

One of our favorite books. *Alexander and The Terrible, Horrible, No Good, Very Bad Day.* I used to love saying that. When you are having such a day, reciting that book title makes you smile, a little at least.

I'm sorry you're sad. I'm not, so that's something to be grateful for, isn't it? Or maybe I should be sad to have died too young? Although who's to say what is "too young." Am I angry about it? No. I chose a Russian roulette lifestyle. No regrets.

Meanwhile, I opened the manual one more time. TAKE TO THE SKY. Finally, something I understand.

I tried to see what was next, but even though the manual looks thick, I couldn't turn the page.

What should I wear the day I'm finally ready to fly? I'd like to have a cape. But what kind? Superman red? Gauzy pink? Black velvet? Is velvet too heavy to fan out behind me? And what type of clothes accent a cape?

Lots to consider, fashion-wise.

Maybe I'm a ghost. Maybe I can visit you. I'll try to let you know in advance, so I don't scare you. I don't think I'll look like Casper, but you never know.

You. Never. Know. That piece of wisdom should be in their manual!

Love, Hilee in the Skies with Rhinestones

Dear Hilee,

I woke up thinking about the patterns that are still gripping me and wondering how I will free myself of them. I thought I could keep you safe. Then I thought, when I got older, you could help keep me safe. Two daughters—enough to help me through old age.

When I realized you probably couldn't "be there for me," I still thought that in an emergency, you could sit by me, you could comfort Sarah.

Despite all my blessings, these last two weeks have been sad. I wake up sad. I think about you, write about you, feel the sorrow. I miss having two living daughters. I feel unbalanced, unsafe. How does a person survive such a loss?

You are probably thinking, *Sarah is the good daughter. How could Mom even begin to think I'd be helpful?*

These are my gloomy thoughts this morning. Now I should follow your sage advice: "Nothing matters, ha ha ha." Even writing that makes me smile. And now, a daughter who's taking to the skies! Things are literally looking up.

Love, Mom

Dear Mom,

It's distressing reading your gloomy thoughts. Maybe that's how you felt about my depression all those years—a web of dank and darkness thrown over you. Part of me thinks, *Really Mom, can't a dead girl rest in peace?* A small part of me wants to be more compassionate. This is the unbearable freedom of being dead—it's a callous liberation.

Anyhow, I'm flattered you thought I might be helpful if you got sick, since I was such a general fuckup about showing up for anything. But Mom, you are always the most hopeful person.

Love, Hilee

May, Mother's Day
Minus One

Years ago, Hilee opted out of Mother's Day. She usually managed to leave me a voicemail or text during the late afternoon of that Sunday. Sarah and Jeff always balloon my spirits by creating a lovely meal for us all. Even though months have passed since Hilee's death, I still feel unbalanced, unsafe, having only one living daughter. I still freeze inside when someone asks, "How many children do you have?" But I have trained myself to say "Two." If someone asks further questions, I tell them about Hilee and our letters. So far, each person is intrigued by the concept.

Dear Hilee,

I struggle with the idea that I will never see you again. It's an untenable thought and I shove it away so I can function. I can laugh and joke and carry on conversations and sometimes write and go to the grocery store. From the outside, I seem like a well-adjusted, older woman. But inside, I am a pot of sorrow ready to spill. I know you're dead—you wouldn't be writing to me if you weren't—but I cannot accept the finality of your death. It's heavy, heavy, heavy inside me, even when I appear to feel fine.

Sadly, Mom

Dear Mom,

I am so sorry I caused you such heartache.

But I have news—I can fly! Only a little. But still, I was airborne for twenty-five seconds and it was divine. Soon you'll be able to point up into the sky (I'm assuming I am above you) and say, "It's a bird. It's a plane. It's Hilee!"

Love, Super Hilee

Dear Hilee,

Two grieving mothers talk about their dead daughters. That's what my ailing friend Judith and I are doing. As I mentioned earlier, her daughter died six months before you did. Judith and I have so many parallels in our lives. Now, she is dying of bladder cancer. She is sanguine and accepting: "Getting her affairs in order," as they say. She is thoughtful and organized and is giving away her clothes and household items to programs that help impoverished women.

"If I have a miracle cure, I'll have to buy new clothes," she says.

"You'll have fun doing it," I say.

Judith and I talk about our sorrow and also about a sense of relief. For years, we've been on tenterhooks, worrying that we'd get a phone call in the middle of the night.

Oh wait, I did get that phone call. And it was every bit as terrifying as I had imagined. Maybe worse. That was the last call your cellphone made—Matthew telling me you weren't breathing.

Hilee, I am only sad part of the time. Much of the time I am my usual self, with just an undertow of sadness.

Meanwhile, hooray for meeting your goal. "It's a bird. It's a plane. It's Super Hilee!"

Love, Mom

Dear Mom,

I'm wondering if I am turning into an angel. I certainly don't have the outfit: No wings, no halo, no white robe or beatific smile. But isn't that one of the options when you die? Or must you do a lot of good deeds and be a stellar citizen to reach angel status?

I am probably just a dead person. Period. Which is fine.

However, I see that you're not fine, and I wish I could pop down for a surprise visit. Honestly, though, I don't know how.

Every so often, I drift into introspection and wish I'd been a better sister, aunt, daughter, friend, citizen. But when those regretful thoughts march into my mind, I bat them away. I've had enough of beating myself up.

Alive, I heard a lot of talk from various therapists urging "forgiveness." But I liked holding a grudge and "suffering." I liked plotting revenge on those who had wronged me.

Now, none of that matters. Could be forgiveness. Could be indifference.

But I'm starting to see how much you and Sarah totally loved me and were trying to help me. Maybe you didn't love her best after all: maybe you loved us both. It chokes me up to let that in, although maybe it's because my cigarette smoke went down crooked. Remember, you gave me permission to smoke, and I am not one to ignore such an invitation.

Did you know that once I learn to keep aloft, I get to throw myself off a pretend cliff as part of flight training? I'm pretty excited because it's such a dramatic, impulsive, self-destructive gesture—like I'll be committing suicide. But it's literally for a "higher purpose." Ha ha ha. Pretty good one, eh Mom?

For that occasion, I'm going to wear black velvet and carry a book of dark verses from Edgar Allen Poe.

See how essential **Poe** is to the foundation of **poe**try!

Love, Hilee

Dear Hilee,

I am torn—I want to keep writing to you, to hear your voice, to stay connected. And I also want to move on, to write about something else that's not so emotional and sad. How will we know when we've written enough? How will I keep my feeling of connection with you?

Mother's Day today. Not your favorite holiday. We wouldn't have been together, but you probably would have given me a late afternoon call. In two more months, I will have been through every holiday without you. On July 20th, an entire year will have passed. Hard to believe.

Ron and I listened to a man talk about the power of integrating death into life, of learning what death has to teach us about living fully. Ever since you died, I think about death so much more.

We had dinner with cousin Janet and I talked about how I missed you. Janet misses you as well. She looked back at her old calendar and discovered she had taken you to the grocery store, the doctor, the pharmacy, three or four times a week, almost every week. She was such a vital part of your life and of our lives. And still is!

Ron and I were watching *Ted Lasso*, a comedy that is getting too serious for my taste. A mother said to her grown daughter, "I keep your room the way it was when you were a girl to remind me of the time when we were close."

I burst into tears and couldn't stop sobbing. So many things cause me to cry these days.

Love, Mom

Dear Mom,

Whoa, that's bad news if you're crying during comedies. But I know what you mean. When the tears are there, any trigger can make them pour out.

Mom, I don't have any advice. Maybe I'm too fascinated by my new self to concentrate on you. But I've always been like that, haven't I? I'm not ashamed of it.

Remember when Dad used to say, "I'll be dead someday and you'll be sorry you didn't love me enough."

He's dead. I'm dead. I loved him a lot—maybe too much—but I'm not sorry I didn't love him more. Mom, you need to stop thinking about me so much, have more fun. You know that, don't you?

Here's the good news. I am fine. You don't have to worry about me anymore. You know where to find me and I promise to answer any letter relatively promptly. At least within seven to ten business days. There's nothing to stew over, as far as I am concerned.

I am without expectation. Someone suggests I take deep breaths so I can manifest tattoos. I try it. Someone tells me to jump up and down so I can learn to fly. I jump, even if I'm wearing high-heeled boots. Someone offers me a toke—I gratefully inhale. A cigarette? I savor the smoke. If drugs or alcohol or Diet Coke or candy bars appear, I welcome them. Because I am invincible. A superwoman who doesn't have to save anyone. Not even herself.

Now, I'm off for another try at flying. Anna Wintour, famous *Vogue* Editor-in-Chief, please note: I am wearing cherry-red velveteen hot pants! A midnight blue vest. And a fetching short magenta cape, that flutters around my shoulders. Plus, cherry-colored pumps. The shoes may fall off while I fly but that's just one of the hazards of being ultra-chic.

Don't you wish you had such an outfit? Only, instead of hot pants you'd wear trousers with pockets, right?

Love, Hilee

Dear Hilee,

I am trying to imagine myself in cherry red velveteen trousers, my hands jauntily in my pockets. Yes, please send me a pair in size ten.

Even when I go for days without writing to you, I carry you around in my head. We drive past a Sonic and I think about your Route 66 Happy Hour Special, no ice. We eat at Applebee's, and I imagine how you would have loved our waiter with tattooed arms, pompadour hairstyle, and a T-shirt advertising *Late Night Appetizers*. I walk on a steep trail in the riparian forest (Yes, I put in "riparian" to see if you were paying attention. It is a forest near a lake or river.) and think you'd avoid this hike at all costs and wait in the car, on your cellphone. I see a cardinal, a leather jacket, a girl with purple hair, and I think of you.

Yesterday, I saw a plane cruising low over Loose Park. Someday, I'll look up and see you overhead. You'll be smiling because you'll have taken to the skies.

You'll be flying high, dear Hilee, just like you deserve.

Love, Mom

June/July, as the Anniversary of Hilee's Death Approaches

During these months, I read and reread our letters. I mourn the irrevocable loss of my daughter and I celebrate our new relationship. It's a pattern I'm getting used to: the inescapable rollercoaster of reveling in my blessings and sorrowing over what I've lost.

Dear Hilee,

The anniversary date of your death is looming. If you're considering a resurrection, July 20th is an ideal date.

When I started going to the grief therapist, I told her I wanted to knock down the internal wall that I had created in order to stay connected with you. I loved you so much, (I still love you) and yet I couldn't show you my deep feelings because you'd mock me or try to manipulate me or get angry for random reasons. Expressing my love for you didn't feel safe.

All this month, I have been quite emotional, crying at the slightest provocation—I even cried during a laughter group I was facilitating! When I told Eve about my jags of sadness, she said, "I guess the wall is gone."

Hilee, the wall is gone. I still don't believe you are dead, but I am more in touch with my everyday sorrow. It's a relief. How can I have existed without you for this many months? I didn't know it was possible. I didn't know I could do it. Thank goodness we found a way to stay connected. I'm not sure you needed it, but I did.

And writing all these letters helped me realize we are always connected. No matter how or if we communicate, you are woven through my heart and soul. You have been since the day you were born, and you will be until I die and beyond.

Sending love, Mom

Dear Mom,

Something is changing here. I feel I should pack my bag for a journey. Of course, I don't have a bag or anything to put in it. I don't have a passport or photo ID. But I feel like I might be relocating soon. Back to Kansas? Higher up in the sky? Time travel to Medieval days? Who knows?

When I really master flying, when I make friends with clouds, hitch rides on the gulf stream, and cozy up to migrating birds to get directions, guess who I'm coming to visit? You! And Sarah! And the rest of our family.

But you might not know I'm there until I get back here and write to you. So, you may as well decide I'm always with you!

Love, Hilee

Dear Hilee,

I am reading your letters. What a wit you have, what a breadth of knowledge. You are a Renaissance woman, with a swath of hedonism. As I read, I laugh, then go misty. You are you, with the prickles, shackles, and hustles of life on Earth. Sometimes I feel like I'm sitting in a pool of love for you, all the rough edges gone, all the hurts and irritants dissipated, that pure wrenching motherly love I experienced when you were a baby.

You've been dead for a year. How bitter. How odd. How devastating. How unbelievable. How life-changing. How deeply sorrowful. And yet, during the times we are writing letters, our connection has felt so playful, so real, so strong. What a gift. What a surprise. What a healing.

Love, Mom

Section III

Getting Through the First Year

Things That Helped

I talked, I wrote, I listened.

I talked about Hilee's death. I went on walks with friends and told the story. When friends kindly said, "I don't know if you feel like talking about it..." I said, "I want to talk about it."

I wrote about Hilee's death, pouring out the raw and terrible facts. I documented other details of the days and weeks after Hilee died; they crowded my mind and I wanted to remember them.

I listened to people talk about their own grief. Of course, I was familiar with the stages of grieving, and I had mourned the deaths of many family members and friends. But this experience, my child's death, was different. Hilee's death impaled me, infuriated me, eroded me. As I listened to others, I saw that my numbness, disbelief, confusion, denial, and wrenching sadness were all parts of this journey. Their stories soothed and inspired me, giving me much needed permission to grieve in the way most natural to me.

I cried

I let my tears spill whenever they came. The grocery store, the dermatologist's office, on a walk, during a Zoom call. I once cried while I was leading a Zoom Laughter Yoga class. When I was alone, I keened, I wailed, I pounded pillows, I roared. I threw myself into my sorrow like the worn-out woman I was.

I talked to other parents.

I reached out to a few support groups, desperate to be in the company of others who had lost their children, particularly to drugs. Their kindness, openness, ideas for coping, and honesty at discussing these monumental losses helped me breathe more deeply.

I searched for answers, then I let go of my questions.

I didn't know my daughter was using hard drugs and I yearned to find out the details: How did she get the money to pay for them? Why were there so many needles in her home? How long had she been using? Why had she started?

I'd wake up in the night, questions clawing at me. I reached out to her boyfriend, but he had little to say. Likewise with the few other friends of hers I was able to find. My daughter led an intricate, private life and after many sleepless nights, the "Let It Go," song from *Frozen* floated into my head. I let it go.

I accepted all help.

Hilee adored receiving, but I always felt more comfortable giving. During the gut punch of Hilee's sudden death, I was not my normal generous self: I was a robot with uncoiled hinges. People brought me food, sent me inspirational cards and healing gifts, visited me, called me, and called me again when I was incapable of reaching out.

I gratefully accepted everything.

I treated myself like I would treat a grieving friend.

I let go of judgements and allowed myself time and space to grieve. I admitted to friends, "I seem unable to make a phone call right now. Can you reach out to me?" They instantly understood, assuaging my guilt at not being a "good friend." I didn't berate myself for my lack of productivity. I let my feelings flow, often saying to Ron things like: "I can't cook right now." Or "I can't watch anything suspenseful or about death or drugs on TV." Or, "I can't concentrate." He listened and supported me in every way he could.

I admitted I was lost, and I found a grief therapist.

"I need help," I told people. "I'd like a therapist, but I don't have the energy to find one."

When my friend Marie heard this, she said, "I know someone you will love." A week later I had an appointment. Three weeks later, my therapist suggested I write Hilee letters. And have Hilee write me back. That idea changed my life.

Section IV

Coda

Dear Reader,

As I near the two-year anniversary of Hilee's death, I feel a need to connect with her, to hear her voice. These are some of our final letters to each other, so far.

Dear Hilee,

I like celebrating your birthdate, but I don't like acknowledging your death date.

Remember how you always got sad and gloomy before Larry's death day. I am now like that around your death day; not as openly sad and dramatic as you were, as that is not in my nature, but internally grieving, grieving, grieving.

Where are you and what are you doing? It's the same question Annabelle asks when we're out of town. She likes to keep track of her family members. So do I.

Love, Mom

Dear Mom,

I'm glad you haven't forgotten me. We talk about that up here; what if everyone on earth forgets we ever existed. Some of my dead friends have almost no family. Or what family they had, they've totally alienated. Hmmm, wonder how that happened. They stew over it, why I'm not sure. But maybe I don't understand them because I know at least a few people remember me. I tried to alienate you all, didn't I?

Things look a little different around here. Before there were streaks of pinkness and cheer. Now it's grayer, more cloudy. Suits me.

I find myself in a group of discards, drug users mainly—you can't really say "former drug users," because we'd like to still be using. So, unrepentant drug users are my friends. A little like home, only without the sensible interference from well-meaning family and friends. So, it's a laissez-faire group of outcasts and we mostly get along.

But Mom, the place is becoming like a psych ward in the sky. One of the angels, who describes himself as a "former addict," flies overhead every couple of days, like an old-timey crop duster, spewing out 12-step type information. Maybe they're hoping to reform us so they can recycle us back to Earth. After all this rambling, Mom, the most important thing is, DO NOT FORGET ME! Tell Sarah, too, okay? I know I can count on you guys, "on earth as it is in heaven."

Pretty Biblical, huh!

Love, Hilee

Dear Hilee,

Don't worry. I will never forget you.

Love, Mom

Dear Hilee,

The shirt I bought for myself, with your approval, on our last thrift store visit, is getting shabby. Do I give it away or keep it hanging in my closet forever? I'm voting for the closet right now. I have one of your gorgeous sundresses, which I am never going to wear, in my other closet. It has been there for two years, taking up psychic space, when it could be giving someone delight. But when I touch it, I can't get rid of it. I have your ashes. I have your leather jacket. What are your thoughts about these remnants?

Love, Mom

Dear Mom,

Thanks for keeping some of my clothes. Most of them were trash. But the ones my former boyfriend Greg bought me were really wonderful. Remember my Chanukah dress, midnight blue with lots of twinkling stars. So amazing! Equally amazing, the man was trying to turn me into someone I was not. I let him try. I was curious—maybe I could be that charming submissive creature he so wanted and needed. I should have known better. Well, actually, I did know better, but I went along for the clothes, the trinkets, and the ride. Part fun, part oppression. At least the fun was in there. I was a big old fat girl. Then, after my by-pass surgery,

I was a skinny girl with a lot of extra skin. Not as glamorous as I had expected, but still, worth it! Worth it to escape from the weight of the world on my bones. I gussied up pretty good, didn't I?

Mom, whatever you decide on the clothes is fine with me. As you know, I can now envision any outfits I want. Right now, I am dressing as a cat burglar. It suits me as I feel I'm tiptoeing around the edges of life and death, stumbling over both and not particularly good at either one.

Love, Hilee, Daughter of the Dark

Dear Mom,

The other day, as some of us were sitting around, talking about Life on Earth, an angel flew by and said, "Silence everyone. God's walking around."

"God? What do you mean, God?" I said.

Rock looked at me, eyebrows raised, shaking his head. "I know you're a heathen or something like that, but you have heard of God? Right?"

"Oh, god yes."

Rock laughed, though not everyone thought it was funny.

But seriously, I wanted to know, what did that mean, *God's walking around*. Did God turn out to be a corporeal being after all?

Before I could ask questions, everything went silent and gray, like we were suddenly in a vacuum. No one spoke. Then light was everywhere, so bright that I had to close my eyes. Everything shook, like the giant in *Jack and the Beanstalk* was stomping around. But it wasn't scary like an earthquake. It was surprisingly peaceful. An unusual feeling of relaxation came over me. I thought, *If God came by more often, we probably wouldn't be chatting about drugs so much.* Then the light was gone, and we all just looked at each other. Wow. And started talking about drugs again.

Love, Hilee

Dear Hilee,

What an experience. Too bad you didn't get to see God.

Love, Mom

Dear Mom,

I didn't need to see God. I saw the light. Isn't that enough?

Love, H

Dear Hilee,

Did you learn anything from seeing that massive light?

Love, Mom

Dear Mom.

I learned I need a better pair of sunglasses. No wonder God is depicted as alone in the firmament. (Aha! How do you like that vocabulary word—firmament. Wouldn't that be an amazing Scrabble coup?)

Seriously, all that shining and shaking would really hinder any sort of meaningful communication. That's probably what happened with my wayward relationships—I held too much light. And my anxiety was savage. I was always fiddling and shaking and clomping my knee up and down. Hence the reach out to medications and drugs to calm me the fuck down.

Love, Hilee Om

Dear Hilee,

It is less than a week before my birthday, exactly one week until my session with Molly, the seer, and eight days from the two-year anniversary of your death. Not that I'm keeping track. From what you have told me, your death was not traumatic for you, but rather a losing of time, a drifting away. I still can't really think of it without feeling sick.

Love, Mom

Dear Mom,

Talk about trading places. The two years of being dead has been easy breezy for me, while you've been agonizing half of the time. I used to envy you, but only a little, for your cheerfulness. Of course, that cheerfulness was also quite irritating. I felt like you didn't care about me: you were functioning and making your way through life, and I was so so sad and depressed and dark in a hole of despair. But in retrospect, if we'd both been mired in misery, I couldn't have had my meds, my food, so many of the practical things I now realize you made happen.

Love, Hilee

Dear Hilee,

Two years ago at this time, you were still alive. This morning, I read some of our texts from that time. It was sweet reading them. Lots of logistics, re picking up meds and food, along with texts about how anxious you are, how crazy you're feeling.

Your texts were rather civilized. Your phone calls were more chaotic and angry. If you reread our texts, perhaps you'd notice what an interesting person you are. Even in your down, down days, you are looking for sparks— flamingo head bobbles, leopard print skirts—to bring you cheer. That's something we have in common. I am always looking for splashes of cheer and even more now that you are dead.

Love, Mom

Dear Mom,

Yes, we both like silly little things. Why not? They're fun.

Mom, here's the thing. I can't even remember if I was alone when I decided to take the drugs that night. Usually, I only did pot when I was by myself. Not out of safety concerns. Of course not. Just because pot seemed more solitary, more medicinal. The real stuff was more serious, something I wanted to make the most of. Anyhow, I don't remember that last evening. Yes, you and I texted about the phone. Then, I thought about making dinner, probably something with hamburger and cheese and canned tomatoes. You may be thinking, "Why didn't she make him dinner? Maybe she would still be alive?" That is a giant maybe, Mom. Aren't you a person who semi-believes "everyone is on their perfect path?" Although you never believed I was on my perfect path—you kept trying to help me get back on that invisible yellow brick road. Don't worry— I'm not criticizing you.

Maybe I'm part of a little-known group called *The Ungrateful Dead?* I'm dead. I'm generally not a big "count your blessings" kind of gal. I wish I had the T-shirt.

Anyway, happy Day of the Dead, Mom. Let's have as much fun as possible, shall we?

Love, Hilee

Dear Hilee,

Let's do have fun. Dan is taking Ron and me to Cascone's for a Hilee Memorial Meal. How do you like that? I love you, Hilee. Always and forever. Grateful or ungrateful. Dead or alive.

Love, Mom

Section V

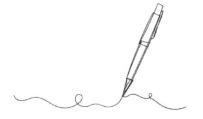

Turning the Page

Dear Hilee,

What would you think if I turned our letters into a book? One day I think *yes*, another day I think *no*. Do you have any suggestions?

Love, Mom

Dear Mom,

I am just sitting here, calm and ever ready, waiting for someone like you to ask for advice. Don't worry so much. The book is going to happen. The people who need it will read it.

I have to admit that sounds suspiciously like something you would say to me. Oh no, I'm turning into my mother! Although most people don't wait until they're dead to do that.

Love, Hilee

Acknowledgments

How could I have written this book without my friends and family and without the immense kindness of my writing community?

My daughter Sarah and I walked and talked and walked and talked, trying to make sense of this terrible loss. She was an immense comfort, as were her children, my grandchildren, and her husband Jeff.

Writing this book was very emotional, and my life partner Ron nurtured me during so many times of depression, irritability, and hopelessness. He also gallantly read aloud the book to me, twice, and was an integral part of my editing process.

My critique partners, Andrea and Barbara, Jacqueline, Judith, and Robin, were essential to the emergence of this book. It's not easy to edit the work of a grieving friend and they worked with kindness, empathy, and honesty, reading every letter, making important suggestions and corrections, encouraging me all along the way.

My brother Dan and his partner Dena offered me vital affirmations, reading the manuscript, offering well-honed suggestions, and cradling me in my grief. Dan's weekly visits, along with phenomenal baked goods (chocolate, of course) were an essential part of my grieving and healing experience.

My dear friend Maril read every word and offered insightful critiques and endless emotional support. My nephew Jake offered meaningful edits as I completed this writing journey.

Marie not only guided me to my grief therapist but also volunteered to read the letters. Her insights were invaluable. Ruth-Ann generously offered feedback in the midst of her own grief,

My beloved Kansas City Writers Group is always a source of inspiration, encouragement, and comfort. They showered me with thoughtful gifts and deep caring. The Dottie Memorial Breakfast Club friends were also a source of inspiration and encouragement.

My KCWG co-facilitator Mary-Lane read the letters after I was "done" and showed me a myriad of ways to improve the work. Throughout the process, she was a tireless cheerleader.

Patti read the book as a friend and as a professional who counsels grieving people. Her suggestions shone and when she asked if she could share the manuscript with a client, I was beyond delighted.

Special thanks for the parental grief groups that so

generously welcomed me. I'm grateful to Cindy, another grieving parent, who read the book and offered me guidance and comfort.

I am eternally grateful to my grief therapist, for her letter-writing idea, and for her patience, humor, empathy, wisdom, and guidance.

I couldn't have functioned without my heroic relatives—Zach, Jake, Janet, Char, Jeff, and Dan, along with the emotional support of Brian, Helen, Myrna, Sonya, and Renee, who rushed to the rescue and helped with vital practical matters and empathetic listening after Hilee's death.

Thank you for anyone else who helped me that I neglected to mention. My gratitude is boundless.

About Deborah

Deborah Shouse, Kansas City, Missouri, enjoys the flexibility, humility, excitement, connections, and joy inherent in the writing life.

She has been featured in many anthologies, including more than five-dozen *Chicken Soup* books. For years, she wrote a Love Story column for *The Kansas City Star*. Deborah and her life partner Ron Zoglin co-wrote *Antiquing for Dummies* and she co-authored several volumes in the *Yes, You Can* financial series.

Deborah has worked with and written about people who are living with dementia and their care partners. She authored two books on this subject: *Love in the Land of Dementia: Finding Hope in the Caregiver's Journey* and *Connecting in the Land of Dementia: Creative Activities to Explore Together*. Working with medical professionals and care partners, Deborah and Ron have presented their stories and ideas in countries such as New Zealand, England, Chile, Costa Rica, India, Italy, and Turkey.

After writing hundreds of articles, essays, and short stories, dozens of books, plus a myriad of editing and ghost-writing projects, Deborah lived out a long-time dream: writing a novel. *An Old Woman Walks Into a Bar*.

Shortly after completing her novel, Deborah experienced a life-altering tragedy: her older daughter Hilee died from a drug overdose. Writing *Letters from the Ungrateful Dead: A Grieving Mom's Surprising Correspondence with Her Deceased Adult Daughter* was an integral part of Deborah's healing journey.

If this book resonates, she'd love to hear from you: DeborahShouseWrites.com

Made in United States
North Haven, CT
23 September 2024

57785469R00129